1

Comfortably casual in
a plain jersey, topped
with a matching
striped jerkin. Gay in
contrasting colours; chic
in closely related shades
as shown here.

Knit
Sizes 32-40 inch bust.

2

*Just unfasten the
fashionably laced front
of this top before
you put it on, and
even the most elaborate
hair-do will survive!
The set-in sleeves
are delightfully
bell-shaped. All in all,
the prettiest tunic yet.*

*Knit
Sizes 32-40 inch bust.*

3

*Far right Cable and rib
panels for a casual,
country look, with an
interesting saddle-top
shoulder. Add
two stripes of colour
at the neck and cuffs,
and you've a smart
co-ordinate to match
with either skirt
or pants.*

*Knit
Sizes 32-40 inch bust.*

Happy Birthday
Joan.
Love
Holly

ALL YOU CAN
KNIT & CROCHET
FOR WOMEN

Marshall Cavendish

CONTENTS

Published by Marshall Cavendish Books Limited
58 Old Compton Street
London W1V 5PA

© Marshall Cavendish Limited 1972 – 84

Printed and bound in Italy by
New Interlitho SpA.

ISBN 0 86307 218 6

This volume is not to be sold in Australia,
New Zealand or North America

Edited by Pam Dawson

Photographs by Camera Press (Femina-Design) Nos 1, 2, 6, 11, 27, 38. GMN 4, 9, 17, 24, 31, 42. Arne Nilsson 7. Uggla 8. Kamerabild 14, 21, 22, 37, 41. Neal Walder 23. Ed-Foto 20. Jan Ralf 25, 26, 33. Lars Larsson 44. Simis Press 3, 5, 10, 12, 13, 14, 15, 16, 18, 19, 29, 30, 32. Stephen Hiett 34, 35, 36. Templetons 39, 40. Sandra Lousada 43. John Carter 45.

4

Left Summer flattery in
a delightful boat-neck.
Cotton bouclé and a
textured stocking stitch
go to make up this
useful light-weight jersey.

Knit
Sizes 32-42 inch bust.

5

Right Applied smocking
on bell sleeves is the
outstanding feature of
this eye-catching two-
piece. The dress has a
high ribbed collar, and
the buttoning jacket is
edged with double crochet.

Knit
Sizes 32-38 inch bust.

6

Superb styling for town
or country. A jersey
suit with polo neck top,
and a midi skirt you can
adjust to any length.

Knit
Sizes 34-40 inch bust.

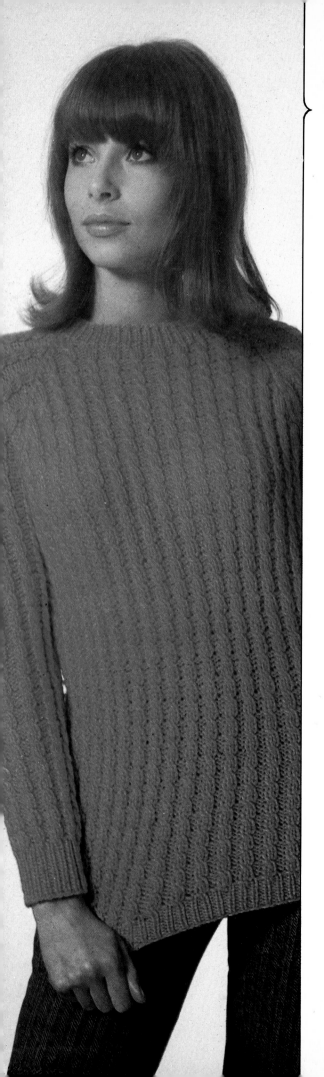

7

Left A simple mock cable stitch, and raglan sleeves allowing plenty of movement, make this an ideal sports sweater.

Knit
Sizes 32-40 inch bust.

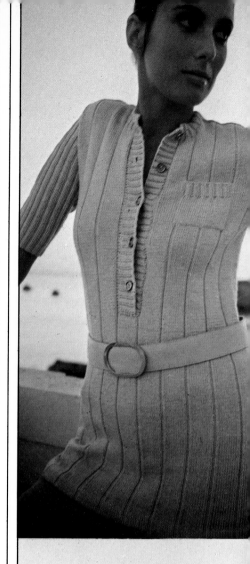

8

Top right Get a good slim fit with this long ribbed jersey. Front buttoning gives extra fashion interest.

Knit
Sizes 34-40 inch bust.

9

Right Feminine and highly flattering— that's this lacy blouse with long bishop sleeves.

Knit
Sizes 34-40 inch bust.

10

Far right Colourful random stripes, a neat collar and ribbed cuffs—all add up to a bold, well-shaped shirt.

Knit
Sizes 34-42 inch bust.

11

Far left Look casual yet elegant in this long-line cardigan. Special feature—a textured arrowhead effect, easily worked in single rib.

Knit
Sizes 34-40 inch bust.

12

Left Crochet with a raised, ribbed effect— that's the basis of this highly versatile long-line cardigan. There's a particularly wide size range too.

Crochet
Sizes 34-44 inch bust.

13

Right A charming midi to crochet. Bell sleeves, a cord fastening and contrasting bands of colour at the hem complete the design.

Crochet
Sizes 34-42 inch bust.

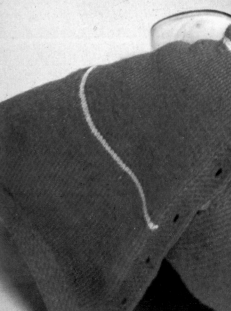

16

*Right A casual
car coat, with
comfortable raglan
sleeves and roomy
pockets. Contrasting
bands of colour on all
edgings make it
come alive!*

*Knit
Sizes 34-42 inch bust.*

17

*A casual classic that's
easy to wear.
This charming cardigan
suit has a wide-ribbed
button-through jacket
and plain stocking
stitch skirt.*

*Knit
Sizes 34-40 inch bust.*

18, 19

Left Crochet traditionally
spells femininity.
The matching jersey
and cardigan can be
worked in a wide
range of sizes.

Crochet
Sizes 32-50 inch bust.

20

*Work the motifs
singly. Then make them
up into the appealing
matching jacket and
beret.*

*Crochet
Sizes 34-36 inch bust.*

21, 22

Right For a beautiful
summer outfit, crochet
this sleeveless cotton
dress and matching
casual cover-up.
Special features—the
elegant tie belt and
three-quarter sleeved
jacket.

*Crochet
Sizes 34-40 inch bust.*

23

Far left An up-to-the-minute 'square' design! Choose your colour combination. Then make up the granny square cardigan piece by piece.

*Crochet
Sizes 34-36 inch bust.*

24

Left A handy slip-on. Work the stripes in vibrant colours or toning shades.

*Knit
Sizes 32-38 inch bust.*

25,26

Bottom left Bring some pop-art into your wardrobe with these two exciting slip-ons. One features suggestive red lips; the other, a striking star.

*Knit
Sizes 32-36 inch bust.*

27

There's a wide range of sizes in this elegant lace-panelled jerkin and matching, cleverly-shaped skirt.

*Knit
Sizes 34-42 inch bust.*

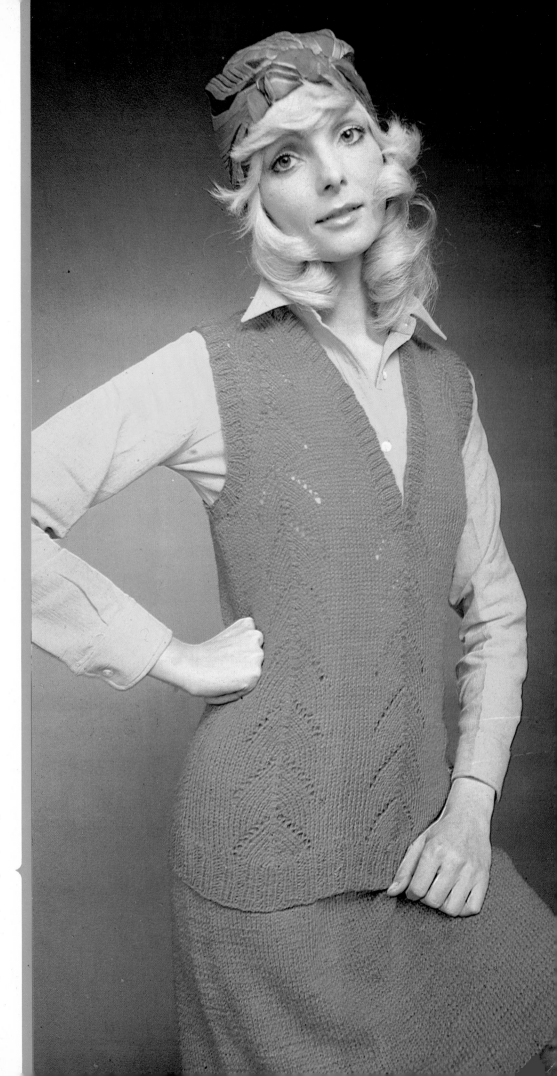

28

To crochet : a beach-wear stunner ! The set comprises a well-fitting bikini and long, sleeveless jacket to match.

Crochet
Sizes 32-38 inch bust.

29

Another glamorous beach outfit. Cool bikini with co-ordinating cover-up.

Crochet
Sizes 32-36 inch bust.

30

Accessorise your beach outfit with this Garbo hat and matching bag in shiny raffia.

Crochet
Size Average head.

31

Right Soft and feminine—that's how you'll feel in this mohair sleeveless top with face-flattering cowl neck.

Knit
Sizes 32-40 inch bust.

32

Centre A delightful diagonal-patterned classic with short sleeves. Wear it under a suit, or as a top over a skirt or slacks.

Knit
Sizes 32-40 inch bust.

33

Far right A neatly fitting jersey worked in double rib. The v-neck insert and high warm polo collar are worked separately and then sewn into place.

Knit
Sizes 32-38 inch bust.

34

*Traditional Aran
stitches, a shaped waist,
and slits front and back
make this a tunic with
a difference.*

*Knit
Sizes 34-42 inch bust.*

35

*A jaunty beret
and scarf to cheer you
in even the very coldest
Winter wind.*

*Knit
Size Average head.*

36

*A skinny hug-me-tight
to make with or without
sleeves. The matching.
pull-on hat
completes the outfit.*

*Knit
Sizes 32-40 inch bust.
Average head.*

37

Cut a dash in this striking toreador bolero. Work the flower motifs separately. Then join them together to make up the garment.

Crochet
Sizes 34-36 inch bust.

38

Add a touch of romance to a special outfit with this lavishly fringed, triangular shawl. The crocheted squares are bordered with simple chains.

Crochet.

39, 40

Left A button-to-the-neck cardigan and pull-on jersey, both featuring a traditional Fair Isle yoke. Make them up in soft Shetland yarn, in a host of colourways.

Knit
Sizes 34-40 inch bust.

41

Right Easy raglan sleeves, a demure collar and two neat pockets make this the prettiest crocheted coat in town.

Crochet
Sizes 34-40 inch bust.

42

Far right Double-breasted fastenings on the contrasting front panels give this crocheted suit a distinctly naval flavour.

Crochet
Sizes 34-40 inch bust.

43

Top right Elegant evenings in this delicate lacy cardigan with high polo collar. Wear it to button either at the front or back.

*Knit
Sizes 34-38 inch bust.*

44

Bottom right Sparkle all through the evening in this glamorous two-piece cocktail suit, worked in glitter yarn in simple stocking stitch.

*Knit
Sizes 34-42 inch bust.*

1 Jersey and striped sleeveless jacket

Sizes
To fit 32[34:36:38:40]in bust
Jersey length to shoulder, 24[24½:25:25½:26]in
Sleeve seam, 17in
Jacket length to shoulder, 29[29½:30:30½:31]in
The figures in brackets [] refer to the 34, 36, 38 and 40in sizes respectively

Tension
6 sts and 8 rows to 1in over st st worked on No.9 needles

Materials
Jersey 13[14:15:16:17] balls Patons Fiona in main shade, A
Jacket 8[9:9:10:10] balls main shade, A
4[4:5:5:5] balls in contrast colour, B
One pair No.9 needles
One pair No.11 needles
Set of 4 No.11 needles pointed at both ends

Jersey back
Using No.9 needles cast on 98[104:110:116:122] sts.
1st row K14[17:20:23:26] sts, P14, (K14, P14) twice, K14[17:20:23:26] sts.
2nd row P14[17:20:23:26] sts, K14, (P14, K14) twice, P14[17:20:23:26] sts.
These 2 rows form patt. Cont in patt until work measures 4in from beg, ending with a 2nd row.
Keeping patt correct, dec one st at each end of next and every foll 12th row until 88[94:100:106:112] sts rem. Cont without shaping until work measures 17½in from beg, ending with a WS row.
Shape armholes
Cast off 4 sts at beg of next 2 rows. Dec one st at each end of next and foll 5[6:7:8:9] alt rows. 68[72:76:80:84] sts. Cont without shaping until armholes measure 6½[7:7½:8:8½]in from beg, ending with a WS row.
Shape shoulders
Cast off at beg of next and every row 6[6:7:7:7] sts 4 times and 6[7:6:7:8] sts twice. Leave rem sts on holder.

Front
Work as given for back until armhole shaping is completed. Cont without shaping until armholes measure 4½[5:5½:6:6½]in from beg, ending with a WS row.
Shape neck
Next row Patt 26[27:28:29:30] sts, turn and leave rem sts on holder.
Complete this side first. Cast off 2 sts at beg of next and foll alt row, then dec one st at neck edge on every alt row until 18[19:20:21:22] sts rem. Cont without shaping until armhole measures same as back to shoulder, ending at armhole edge.
Shape shoulder
Cast off at beg of next and every alt row 6[6:7:7:7] sts twice and 6[7:6:7:8] sts once.
With RS of work facing, sl first 16[18:20:22:24] sts on holder and leave for centre neck, rejoin yarn to rem sts and patt to end. Complete to match first side, reversing shaping.

Sleeves
Using No.11 needles cast on 42[44:46:48:50] sts.
1st row K0[1:2:3:4] sts, P14, K14, P14, K0[1:2:3:4] sts.
2nd row P0[1:2:3:4] sts, K14, P14, K14, P0[1:2:3:4] sts.
Cont in patt as now set until sleeve measures 1½in from beg. Change to No.9 needles. Cont in patt, inc one st at each end of next and every foll 8th row until there are 70[72:74:76:78] sts. Cont without shaping until sleeve measures 17in from beg, or

required length to underarm, ending with a WS row.
Shape top
Cast off 4 sts at beg of next 2 rows. Dec one st at each end of next and every alt row until 48 sts rem. Cast off at beg of next and every row 2 sts 10 times, 3 sts 4 times and 4 sts twice. Cast off rem 8 sts.

Neckband
Join shoulder seams. Using set of 4 No.11 needles, K across sts on back neck holder, K up 20 sts down side of front neck, K across sts on centre front neck holder and K up 20 sts up other side of neck. 88[92:96:100:104] sts. Work 1½in in rounds of K1, P1 rib. Cast off in rib.

To make up
Press each piece under a damp cloth with a warm iron. Set in sleeves. Join side and sleeve seams. Press seams.

Jacket back
Using No.11 needles and A, cast on 106[112:118:124:130] sts. Beg with a K row work 1½in st st, ending with a K row.
Next row K all sts tbl to mark hemline.
Change to No.9 needles. Beg with a K row cont in st st working throughout in stripes of 20 rows A and 4 rows B. Cont in patt until work measures 4in from hemline, ending with a P row. Dec one st at each end of next and every foll 10th row until 90[96:102:108:114] sts rem. Cont without shaping until work measures 22in from hemline, ending with a P row.
Shape armholes
Cast off 5 sts at beg of next 2 rows. Dec one st at each end of next and foll 5[6:7:8:9] alt rows. 68[72:76:80:84] sts. Cont without shaping until armholes measure 7[7½:8:8½:9]in from beg, ending with a P row.
Shape shoulders
Work as given for jersey back. Cast off rem 32 [34:36:38:40] sts.

Jacket left front
Using No.11 needles and A, cast on 57[60:63:66:69] sts. Work as given for back until work measures 4in from hemline, ending with a P row. Dec one st at beg of next and every foll 10th row until 49[52:55:58:61] sts rem. Cont without shaping until work measures same as back to underarm, less 3in, ending with a P row.
Shape front edge
Dec one st at end of next and every foll 4th row until work measures same as back to underarm, ending at armhole edge.
Shape armhole
Cont to dec at front edge as before, cast off 5 sts at beg of next row. Work 1 row. Dec one st at armhole edge at beg of next and foll 5[6:7:8:9] alt rows. Cont dec at front edge only as before until 18[19:20:21:22] sts rem. Cont without shaping until armhole measures same as back to shoulder, ending at armhole edge.
Shape shoulder
Cast off at beg of next and every alt row 6[6:7:7:7] sts twice and 6[7:6:7:8] sts once.

Jacket right front
Work as given for left front, reversing shaping.

Armbands
Join shoulder seams. Using No.11 needles, A and with RS of work facing, K up 85[91:97:103:109] sts round armhole. Beg 1st row with P1, work in K1, P1 rib for ¾in. Cast off in rib.

Front band
Using No.11 needles and B, cast on 11 sts. Work in K1, P1 rib until band is long enough to fit up right front, round back neck and down left front. Cast off in rib.

To make up
Press as given for jersey. Join side seams. Turn hem to WS and sl st down. Sew on front band. Press seams.

2 Tunic with front lacing

Sizes
To fit 32[34:36:38:40]in bust
Length to shoulder, 25½[26:26½:27:27½]in
Sleeve seam, 17[17:17½:17½:18]in
The figures in brackets [] refer to the 34, 36, 38 and 40in sizes respectively

Tension
6 sts and 8 rows to 1in over st st worked on No.9 needles

Materials
16[17:18:19:20] balls Jaeger Celtic-Spun
One pair No.9 needles
One pair No.11 needles

Back
Using No.11 needles cast on 114[120:126:132:138] sts. Beg with a K row work 1½in st st, ending with a K row.
Next row K all sts tbl to mark hemline.
Change to No.9 needles. Beg with a K row cont in st st until work measures 4in from hemline, ending with a P row.
Shape darts
Next row K1, K2 tog, K36[38:40:42:44] sts, K2 tog, K32[34:36:38:40] sts, sl 1, K1, psso, K36[38:40:42:44] sts, sl 1, K1, psso, K1.
Beg with a P row work 9 rows st st.
Next row K1, K2 tog, K35[37:39:41:43] sts, K2 tog, K30[32:34:36:38] sts, sl 1, K1, psso, K35[37:39:41:43] sts, sl 1, K1, psso, K1.
Dec in same way on foll 10th row. 102[108:114:120:126] sts. Cont without shaping until work measures 18½in from hemline, ending with a P row.
Shape armholes
Cast off 6 sts at beg of next 2 rows.
Next row K1, K2 tog, K to last 3 sts, sl 1, K1, psso, K1.
Next row P to end.
Rep last 2 rows 3[4:5:6:7] times more. 82[86:90:94:98] sts. Cont without shaping until armholes measure 7[7½:8:8½:9]in from beg, ending with a P row
Shape neck and shoulders
Next row Cast off 4[5:5:5:6] sts, K17[17:18:19:19] sts, turn and leave rem sts on holder.
Next row Cast off 2 sts, P to end.
Next row Cast off 4 sts, K to end.
Rep last 2 rows once more, then first of these 2 rows once. Cast off rem 3[3:4:5:5] sts.
With RS of work facing, sl first 40[42:44:46:48] sts on holder and leave for back neck, rejoin yarn to rem sts and K to end. Complete to match first side, reversing shaping.

Front
Work as given for back until front measures 7[7:6½:6½:6]in less than back to underarm, ending with a K row.
Divide for front opening
Next row P50[53:56:59:62] sts, cast off 2 sts, P to end.
Next row K to end, turn and cast on 4 sts. 54[57:60:63:66] sts.
Next row P to end.
Next row K to last 4 sts, sl 1, K3.
Rep last 2 rows for 1½in, ending with a P row.
Next row (eyelet hole) K to last 8 sts, yfwd, K2 tog, K2, sl 1, K3.
Keeping sl st correct on every K row, cont to make eyelet holes in this way at intervals of 1½in from the

previous hole, until work measures same as back to underarm ending at armhole edge.

Shape armhole

Cast off 6 sts at beg of next row. Work 1 row.

Next row K1, K2 tog, patt to end.

Next row Patt to end.

Rep last 2 rows 3[4:5:6:7] times more. Cont without shaping, working eyelet holes as before until 7 in all have been made, then cont for a further 1½in, ending at neck edge. 44[46:48:50:52] sts.

Shape neck

Cast off 3 sts, P to end.

Next row K21[22:23:24:25] sts, turn and leave rem 20[21:22:23:24] sts on holder.

Cast off 2 sts at beg of next and foll 2 alt rows, then cont without shaping until armhole measures same as back to shoulder, ending at armhole edge.

Shape shoulder

Cast off at beg of next and every alt row 4[5:5:5:6] sts once, 4 sts twice and 3[3:4:5:5] sts once.

With RS of work facing rejoin yarn to rem sts, cast on 4 sts, K3, sl 1, K to end. Complete to match first side, reversing shaping and noting that eyelet hole row will be worked as foll: K3, sl 1, K2, sl 1, K1, psso, yfwd, K to end.

Sleeves

Using No.11 needles cast on 49[51:53:55:57] sts.

1st row K1, *P1, K1, rep from * to end.

2nd row P1, *K1, P1, rep from * to end.

Rep these 2 rows for 1¼in, ending with a 2nd row. Change to No.9 needles and cont in st st.

1st row K1[2:3:4:5] sts, (K twice into next st, K4) 9 times, K twice into next st, K2[3:4:5:6] sts. 59[61:63:65:67] sts.

Beg with a P row work 3 rows st st.

5th row K2[3:4:5:6] sts, (K twice into next st, K5) 9 times, K twice into next st, K2[3:4:5:6] sts. 69[71:73:75:77] sts.

Beg with a P row work 3 rows st st.

9th row K2[3:4:5:6] sts, (K twice into next st, K6) 9 times, K twice into next st, K3[4:5:6:7] sts. 79[81:83:85:87] sts.

Beg with a P row work 3 rows st st.

13th row K0[1:2:3:4] sts, (K twice into next st, K6) 11 times, K twice into next st, K1[2:3:4:5] sts. 91[93:95:97:99] sts.

Beg with a P row cont without shaping until sleeve measures 7in from beg, ending with a P row.

Next row K12[13:14:15:16] sts, (K2 tog, K14) 4 times, K2 tog, K to end.

Beg with a P row work 11 rows st st. Cont to dec 5 sts evenly in this way on next and every foll 12th row until 71[73:75:77:79] sts rem. Cont without shaping until sleeve measures 17[17:17½:17½:18]in from beg, ending with a P row.

Shape top

Cast off 6 sts at beg of next 2 rows. Dec at each end of next and every alt row as given for back until 31[33:35:37:39] sts rem. Cast off at beg of next and every row 2 sts 4[4:6:6:6] times and 3 sts 4 times. Cast off rem 11[13:11:13:15] sts.

Neckband

Join shoulder seams. Using No 11 needles and with RS of work facing K across sts of right front neck, K up 18[20:20:22:22] sts up side of front neck, K up 9 sts down back neck, K across sts of back neck, dec one st in centre, K up 9 sts up back neck, K up 18[20:20:22:22] sts down side of front neck and K across sts of left front neck. 133[141:145:153:157] sts. Beg with a 2nd row work 1in rib as given for sleeves.

Cast off in rib.

To make up

Press each piece under a damp cloth with a warm iron. Set in sleeves. Join side and sleeve seams. Turn hem to WS and sl st down. Fold front facings to WS at sl st line and sl st down. Press seams. Make a twisted cord 60in long and thread through eyelet holes to tie at neck edge.

---

3 Jersey with cable panels and saddle-top sleeves

Sizes

To fit 32[34:36:38:40]in bust

Length to shoulder, 22[22½:23:23½:24]in

Sleeve seam, 16½[17:17:17½:18]in

The figures in brackets [] refer to the 34, 36, 38 and 40in sizes respectively

Tension

5¾ sts and 7½ rows to 1in over st st worked on No.8 needles

Materials

12[13:14:15:16] balls Patons Piccadilly in main shade, A

1 ball each in contrast colours, B and C

One pair No.8 needles

One pair No.11 needles

Set of 4 No.11 needles pointed at both ends

Cable needle

Back

Using No.11 needles and A, cast on 102[106:114:118:126] sts.

1st row K2, *P2, K2, rep from * to end.

2nd row P2, *K2, P2, rep from * to end.

Rep these 2 rows 5 times more, inc one st at each end of last row on 34 and 38in sizes only. 102[108:114:120:126] sts. Change to No.8 needles. Commence patt.

1st row P4[5:6:7:8] sts, *K6, P6, K4[5:6:7:8] sts, P6, rep from * 3 times more, K6, P4[5:6:7:8] sts.

2nd row K4[5:6:7:8] sts, *P6, K6, P4[5:6:7:8] sts, K6, rep from * 3 times more, P6, K4[5:6:7:8] sts.

3rd row As 1st.

4th row As 2nd.

5th row P4[5:6:7:8] sts, *sl next 3 sts on to cable needle and hold at front of work, K3 sts, then K3 sts from cable needle – called C6F –, P6, K4[5:6:7:8] sts, P6, rep from * 3 times more, C6F, P4[5:6:7:8] sts.

6th row As 2nd.

7th row As 1st.

8th row As 2nd.

These 8 rows form patt. Cont in patt until work measures 14½in from beg, ending with a WS row.

Shape armholes

Cast off 2 sts at beg of next 2 rows. Dec one st at each end of next and every foll 4th row until 76[80:84:88:92] sts rem, then work 2 rows after last dec ending with a WS row.

Shape shoulders

Cast off 25[25:27:27:29] sts, patt 26[30:30:34:34] sts, cast off rem 25[25:27:27:29] sts. Leave sts on holder for centre neck.

Front

Work as given for back.

Sleeves

Using No.11 needles and B, cast on 50[54:54:58:58] sts. Work 2 rows rib as given for back. Break off B. Join in A, K 1 row, then rib 2 rows. Break off A. Join in C, P 1 row, then rib 1 row. Break off C. Using A only, P 1 row, then cont in rib until sleeve measures 3¼in from beg, ending with a 2nd row and inc one st at each end of last row on 32, 36 and 40in sizes only. 52[54:56:58:60] sts. Change to No.8 needles. Beg with a K row cont in st st, inc one st at each end of 5th and every foll 8th row until there are 72[74:78:80:84] sts. Cont without shaping until sleeve measures 16½[17:17:17½:18]in from beg, ending with a P row.

Shape top

Cast off 2 sts at beg of next 2 rows. 68[70:74:76:80] sts.

Next row K3 sts, K2 tog, K to last 5 sts, sl 1, K1, psso, K3 sts.

Beg with a P row work 3 rows st st.

Cont to dec in this way on next and every foll 4th row 0[1:1:2:2] times more, then on every alt row until 24 sts rem.

Saddle top

Cont in st st without shaping until saddle top measures same as top of shoulder on back and front, ending with a P row. Leave sts on holder.

Neckband

Sew saddle top of sleeves to shoulders of back and front. Using set of 4 No.11 needles, A and with RS of work facing, K across all sts on holders, K2 tog at each seam. Cont in rounds of K2, P2 rib, as foll: Work 2 rounds A. With C, K 1 round, then rib 1 round. With A, K 1 round, then rib 2 rounds. With B, K 1 round, then rib 1 round. Cast off in rib with B.

To make up

Press each piece lightly on WS under a damp cloth with a cool iron. Set in sleeves. Join side and sleeve seams. Press seams.

---

4 Cotton bouclé jersey

Sizes

To fit 32[34:36:38:40:42]in bust

Length to shoulder, 20½[21:21½:22:22½:23]in

Sleeve seam, 12in

The figures in brackets [] refer to the 34, 36, 38, 40 and 42in sizes respectively

Tension

9 sts and 14 rows to 2in over st st worked on No.8 needles

Materials

15[15:16:17:17:18] balls Jaeger Sunlin-Spun

One pair No.8 needles

One pair No.10 needles

Back

Using No.10 needles cast on 76[80:86:90:96:100] sts. Beg with a K row work 9 rows st st.

Next row K all sts tbl to mark hemline.

Change to No.8 needles. Beg with a K row cont in st st until work measures 14in from hemline, ending with a P row.

Shape armholes

Cast off at beg of next and every row 4 sts twice and 2 sts twice. K2 tog at each end of next and foll 1[1:2:2:3:3] alt rows. 60[64:68:72:76:80] sts. Cont without shaping until armholes measure 6½[7:7½:8:8½:9]in from beg, ending with a P row.

Shape shoulders

Cast off 4 sts at beg of next 3 rows.

Next row (neckline) Cast off 4 sts, K to end.

Change to No.10 needles. Beg with a K row work 5 rows st st, inc one st at each end of every row. Cast off.

Front

Work as given for back.

Sleeves

Using No.10 needles cast on 44[46:48:50:52:54] sts. Work hem as given for back. Change to No.8 needles. Beg with a K row cont in st st, inc one st at each end of 5th and every foll 8th row until there are 58[60:62:64:66:68] sts. Cont without shaping until sleeve measures 12in from hemline, ending with a P row.

Shape top

Cast off 4 sts at beg of next 2 rows. K2 tog at each end of next and every alt row until 28 sts rem. Cast off at beg of next and every row 2 sts 6 times and 3 sts twice.

Cast off rem 10 sts.

To make up
Press each piece under a damp cloth with a warm iron. Join shoulder, side and sleeve seams. Set in sleeves. Fold hems at lower edge and neck edge to WS and sl st down. Press seams.

5 Dress with smocked sleeves and sleeveless jacket

Sizes
To fit 32[34:36:38]in bust
34[36:38:40]in hips
Dress length to shoulder, 40[40½:41:41½]in
Sleeve seam, 17[17:17½:17½]in
Jacket length to shoulder, 20[20½:21:21½]in
The figures in brackets [] refer to the 34, 36 and 38in sizes respectively

Tension
7 sts and 9 rows to 1in over st st worked on No.10 needles

Materials
Dress 20[22:24:26] balls Emu Crochet Wool 4 ply
Jacket 6[7:8:9] balls
One pair No.10 needles
One pair No.12 needles
Set of 4 No.12 needles pointed at both ends
One No.2·00 (ISR) crochet hook
Six buttons

Dress back
Using No.12 needles cast on 158[164:172:178] sts. Beg with a K row work 1½in st st, ending with a K row.
Next row K all sts tbl to mark hemline.
Change to No.10 needles. Beg with a K row cont in st st until work measures 5in from hemline, ending with a P row.
Shape darts
Next row K38[40:42:44] sts, sl 1, K1, psso, K to last 40[42:44:46] sts, K2 tog, K to end.
Beg with a P row work 7 rows st st.
Cont to dec in this way on next and every foll 8th row until 110[116:124:130] sts rem. Cont without shaping until work measures 33in from hemline, ending with a P row.
Shape armholes
Cast off at beg of next and every row 5 sts twice and 3[3:4:4] sts twice. Dec one st at each end of next and foll 2[3:4:5] alt rows. 88[92:96:100] sts. Cont without shaping until armholes measure 7[7½:8:8½]in from beg. End with a P row.
Shape shoulders
Cast off at beg of next and every row 8 sts 4 times and 6[7:8:9] sts twice. Leave rem 44[46:48:50] sts on holder.

Dress front
Work as given for back until armhole shaping is completed. Cont without shaping until armholes measure 5[5½:6:6½]in from beg, ending with a P row.
Shape neck
Next row K30[31:32:33] sts, turn and leave rem sts on holder.
Cast off at beg of next and foll alt row 3 sts once and 2 sts once. Dec one st at neck edge on every alt row until 22[23:24:25] sts rem. Cont without shaping until armhole measures same as back to shoulder.
End at armhole edge.
Shape shoulder
Cast off at beg of next and every alt row 8 sts twice and 6[7:8:9] sts once.
With RS of work facing, sl first 28[30:32:34] sts on holder and leave for centre neck, rejoin yarn to rem sts and K to end. Complete to match first side, reversing shaping.

Sleeves
Using No.10 needles cast on 94[96:98:100] sts.
1st row P1[2:3:4] sts, (K1, P6) 13 times, K1, P1[2:3:4] sts.
2nd row K1[2:3:4] sts, (P1, K6) 13 times, P1, K1[2:3:4] sts.
Rep these 2 rows until sleeve measures 2in from beg, ending with a 2nd row. Cont in patt, inc one st at each end of next and every foll 10th row until there are 104[106:108:110] sts. Cont without shaping until work measures 10in from beg, ending with a WS row. Dec one st at each end of next and every alt row until 84[86:88:90] sts rem. Cont without shaping until sleeve measures 17[17:17½:17½]in from beg, ending with a WS row.
Shape top
Cast off 2 sts at beg of every row until 8 sts rem. Cast off.

Neckband
Join shoulder seams. Using set of 4 No.12 needles and with RS of work facing, K across back neck sts, K up 20 sts down side of neck, K across front neck sts and K up 20 sts up other side of neck. Work in rounds of K1, P1 rib for 8in.
Cast off loosely in rib.

To make up
Press each piece under a damp cloth with a warm iron.
Sleeve smocking Beg above cast on edge using blunt ended wool needle and one strand of yarn, join 1st and 2nd K sts tog, take yarn behind work and join 2nd and 3rd K sts tog approx 1in above 2 sts already joined, take yarn behind work again and join 3rd and 4th K sts tog at cast on edge, cont in this way across sleeve. Fasten off. Beg again with 1st and 2nd K ridges 2in from beg and 2nd and 3rd K ridges 3in from beg. Cont in this way until 8 lines of smocking have been worked.
Join side and sleeve seams. Set in sleeves. Turn hem to WS and sl st down. Press seams.

Jacket back
Using No.12 needles cast on 120[126:134:140] sts. Work hem as given for dress back. Change to No.10 needles. Beg with a K row cont in st st until work measures 12in from hemline, ending with a P row.
Shape armholes
Cast off at beg of next and every row 5 sts twice, 4 sts twice and 2[2:3:3] sts twice.
Dec one st at each end of next and foll 4[5:6:7] alt rows. 88[92:96:100] sts. Cont without shaping until armholes measure 8[8½:9:9½]in from beg, ending with a P row.
Shape shoulders
Cast off at beg of next and every row 7 sts 4 times and 6[7:8:9] sts twice. Cast off rem 48[50:52:54] sts.

Jacket left front
Using No.12 needles cast on 62[65:69:72] sts. Work as given for back until front measures same as back to underarm, ending at armhole edge.
Shape armhole and front edge
Next row Cast off 5 sts, K to last 3 sts, K2 tog, K1.
Next row P to end.
Next row Cast off 4 sts, K to end.
Next row P1, P2 tog, P to end.
Next row Cast off 2[2:3:3] sts, K to end.
Next row P to end.
Dec one st at armhole edge on next and foll 4[5:6:7] alt rows, *at the same time* cont to dec at front edge on every 3rd row until 20[21:22:23] sts rem. Cont without shaping until armhole measures same as back to shoulder, ending at armhole edge.
Shape shoulder
Cast off at beg of next and every alt row 7 sts twice and 6[7:8:9] sts once.

Jacket right front
Work as given for left front, reversing all shaping.

To make up
Press as given for dress. Join shoulder and side seams. Turn hem to WS and sl st down. Using No.2·00 (ISR) hook and with RS of work facing, work 2 rounds dc around armholes. Work 2 rows dc up right front edge, round neck and down left front edge, making 6 button loops on right front on 2nd row by working 4ch and missing 4 sts, the first to come 5in above lower edge and the last just below beg of neck shaping, with 4 more evenly spaced between. Press seams. Sew on buttons.

6 Jersey suit with midi skirt

Sizes
To fit 34[36:38:40]in bust
36[38:40:42]in hips
Jersey length to shoulder, 23[23½:24:24½]in
Sleeve seam, 16½[17:17½:18]in
Skirt length, 27½[28:28½:29]in, adjustable
The figures in brackets [] refer to the 36, 38 and 40in sizes respectively

Tension
6 sts and 7½ rows to 1in over st st worked on No.9 needles

Materials
34[36:38:40] balls Lee Target Motoravia Double Knitting
One pair No.9 needles
One pair No.11 needles
Set of 4 No.11 needles pointed at both ends
Waist length of elastic
One 7in zip fastener

Skirt back
Using No.11 needles cast on 77[83:89:95] sts and beg at waist.
1st row K1, *P1, K1, rep from * to end.
2nd row P1, *K1, P1, rep from * to end.
Rep these 2 rows for 1½in, ending with a 2nd row and inc one st at end of last row. 78[84:90:96] sts.
Change to No.9 needles. Beg with a K row work 4 rows st st.
Shape darts
Next row K3 sts, K up 1, K20[22:24:26] sts, K up 1, K32[34:36:38] sts, K up 1, K20[22:24:26] sts, K up 1, K3 sts.
Beg with a P row work 7 rows st st.
Next row K3 sts, K up 1, K21[23:25:27] sts, K up 1, K34[36:38:40] sts, K up 1, K21[23:25:27] sts, K up 1, K3 sts.
Beg with a P row work 7 rows st st.
Cont inc in this way on next and every foll 8th row until there are 110[116:122:128] sts, then on every foll 20th row until work measures 27½[28:28½:29]in from beg, or required length to hem, ending with a K row. Change to No.11 needles.
Next row K all sts tbl to form hemline.
Beg with a K row work 1in st st. Cast off loosely.

Skirt front
Work as given for back.

To make up
Press each piece under a damp cloth with a warm iron. Join side seams leaving 7in open at top of left seam for zip. Sew in zip. Sew elastic inside waist edge with casing st. Turn hem to WS at hemline and sl st down. Press seams.

Jersey back
Using No.11 needles cast on 106[110:118:122] sts.
1st row K2, *P2, K2, rep from * to end.
2nd row P2, *K2, P2, rep from * to end.
Rep these 2 rows for 1½in, ending with a 2nd row and inc one st at each end of last row on 36 and 40in sizes only. 106[112:118:124] sts. Change to

No.9 needles. Commence patt.
1st row K13[16:19:22] sts, P2, K4, P2, (K10, P2, K4, P2) 4 times, K13[16:19:22] sts.
2nd row P13[16:19:22] sts, K2, P4, K2, (P10, K2, P4, K2) 4 times, P13[16:19:22] sts.
These 2 rows form patt. Cont in patt until work measures 16in from beg, ending with a WS row.
Shape armholes
Keeping patt correct, cast off at beg of next and every row 6 sts twice and 2 sts twice. Dec one st at each end of next and foll 5[6:7:8] alt rows. 78[82: 86:90] sts. Cont without shaping until armholes measure 7[7½:8:8½]in from beg, ending with a WS row.
Shape neck and shoulders
Next row Patt 25[26:27:28] sts, turn and leave rem sts on holder.
Next row Cast off 2 sts, patt to end.
Next row Cast off 5 sts, patt to end.
Rep last 2 rows twice more. Work 1 row. Cast off rem 4[5:6:7] sts.
With RS of work facing, sl first 28[30:32:34] sts on holder, rejoin yarn to rem sts and patt to end. Complete to match first side, reversing shaping.

Jersey front
Work as given for back until armhole shaping is completed. Cont without shaping until armholes measure 4½[5:5½:6]in from beg. End with a WS row.
Shape neck
Next row Patt 31[32:33:34] sts, turn and leave rem sts on holder.
Cast off 2 sts at beg of next and foll 2 alt rows. Dec one st at neck edge on every alt row until 19[20:21: 22] sts rem. Cont without shaping until armhole measures same as back to shoulder, ending at armhole edge.
Shape shoulder
Cast off at beg of next and every alt row 5 sts 3 times and 4[5:6:7] sts once.
With RS of work facing, sl first 16[18:20:22] sts on holder and leave for centre neck, rejoin yarn to rem sts, patt to end. Complete to match first side, reversing shaping.

Sleeves
Using No.11 needles cast on 50[50:54:54] sts. Work 3in K2, P2 rib as given for back. Change to No.9 needles. Cont in K2, P2 rib, inc one st at each end of next and every foll 8th row until there are 74[76: 78:80] sts. Cont without shaping until sleeve measures 16½[17:17½:18]in from beg, ending with a WS row.
Shape top
Cast off 6 sts at beg of next 2 rows. Dec one st at each end of next and foll 11[12:13:14] alt rows. 38 sts. Cast off at beg of next and every row 2 sts 8 times and 3 sts 4 times. Cast off rem 10 sts.

Collar
Join shoulder seams. Using set of 4 No.11 needles and with RS of work facing, K across back neck sts on holder, K up 10 sts up side of back neck and 30 sts down side of front neck, K across front neck sts on holder, K up 30 sts up front of neck and 10 sts down back neck. 124[128:132:136] sts. Work in rounds of K2, P2 rib for 8in. Cast off loosely in rib.

To make up
Press as given for skirt. Set in sleeves. Join sides and sleeve seams. Press seams.

7 *Mock cable jersey*

Sizes
To fit 32[34:36:38:40]in bust

Length to centre back, 22[22½:23:23½:24]in
Sleeve seam, 16½[17:17½:17½:18]in
The figures in brackets [ ] refer to the 34, 36, 38 and 40in sizes respectively
Tension
9 sts and 10½ rows to 2in over patt worked on No. 5 needles
Materials
11[12:12:13:14] balls Patons Doublet
One pair No. 5 needles
One pair No. 8 needles
Set of 4 No. 8 needles pointed at both ends

Back
Using No. 8 needles cast on 77[81:85:89:93] sts.
1st row K1, *P1, K1, rep from * to end.
2nd row P1, *K1, P1, rep from * to end.
Rep these 2 rows until work measures 1½in from beg, ending with a 2nd row and inc one st at end of last row. 78[82:86:90:94] sts.
Change to No. 5 needles. Commence mock cable patt.
1st row P2, *put needle behind first st on left hand needle and K 2nd st tbl then K into front of first st and sl both sts off tog – called Cr2 –, P2, rep from * to end.
2nd row K2, *P2, K2, rep from * to end.
3rd row P2, *K2, P2, rep from * to end.
4th row As 2nd.
These 4 rows form patt and are rep throughout.
Cont in patt until work measures 14in from beg, ending with a WS row.
Shape armholes
Cast off 4 sts at beg of next 2 rows. P2 sts tog at each end of next and every alt row until 26[28:30:32:34] sts rem, ending with a WS row. Leave sts on holder.

Front
Work as given for back until 38[40:42:46:48] sts rem, ending with a WS row.
Shape neck
Next row P2 tog, patt 11[11:11:13:13] sts, turn and leave rem sts on holder.
Next row Patt to end.
Next row P2 tog, patt to last 2 sts, P2 tog
Rep last 2 rows until 2 sts rem, ending with a RS row. Cast off.
With RS of work facing, sl first 12[14:16:16:18] sts on holder and leave for centre neck, rejoin yarn to rem sts, P2 tog, patt to end. Complete to match first side.

Sleeves
Using No.8 needles cast on 33[37:37:41:41] sts.
Work in K1, P1 rib as given for back for 2½in, ending with a 2nd row and inc one st at end of last row 34[38:38:42:42] sts
Change to No.5 needles and cont in patt as given for back, inc one st at each end of 7th and every foll 6th row and working extra sts into patt, until there are 62[64:66:68:70] sts. Cont without shaping until sleeve measures 16½[17:17½:17½:18]in from beg, ending with a WS row.
Shape top
Cast off 4 sts at beg of next 2 rows. P2 tog at each end of next and every alt row until 10 sts rem, ending with a WS row. Leave sts on holder.

Neckband
Join raglan seams. Using set of 4 No.8 needles and with RS of work facing K across sts of right sleeve, back neck and left sleeve, K2 tog at each seam, K up 14[14:14:16:16] sts down left side of neck, K across sts of centre front neck and K up 14[14:14:16:16] sts up other side of neck. 84[88:92:98:102] sts. Work in rounds of K1, P1 rib for 1¼in. Cast off in rib.

To make up
Press each piece lightly under a damp cloth with a warm iron. Join side and sleeve seams Press seams.

8 *Long ribbed jersey*

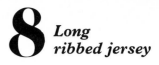

Sizes
To fit 34[36:38:40]in bust
Length to shoulder, 26[26½:27:27½]in
Sleeve seam, 6in
The figures in brackets [ ] refer to the 36, 38 and 40in sizes respectively
Tension
7½ sts and 10 rows to 1in over wide rib patt worked on No. 11 needles
Materials
16[17:17:18] balls Sirdar Fontein Crepe 4 ply
One pair No. 11 needles
One pair No. 13 needles
Five buttons

Back
Using No. 13 needles cast on 142[148:154:160] sts.
Beg with a K row work 1in st st, ending with a K row.
Next row K all sts tbl to form hemline.
Change to No. 11 needles. Commence wide rib patt.
1st row K16[19:16:19] sts, *P2, K10, rep from * to last 18[21:18:21] sts, P2, K16[19:16:19].
2nd row P16[19:16:19] sts, *K2, P10, rep from * to last 18[21:18:21] sts, P2, K16[19:16:19].
These 2 rows form patt. Cont in patt until work measures 3in from hemline, ending with a WS row.
Cont in patt dec one st at each end of next and every foll 20th row until 132[138:144:150] sts rem. Cont without shaping until work measures 19½in from hemline, ending with a WS row.
Shape armholes
Cast off at beg of next and every row 4 sts twice and 3 sts twice. Dec one st at each end of next and every alt row until 106[110:114:118] sts rem. Cont without shaping until armholes measure 6½[7:7½:8]in from beg, ending with a RS row.
Shape neck and shoulders
Next row Patt 42[43:45:46] sts, cast off 22[24:24: 26] sts, patt to end.
Complete right shoulder first.
Next row Cast off 8[8:9:9] sts, patt to end.
Next row Cast off 3 sts, patt to end.
Rep last 2 rows twice more. Cast off rem 9[10:9:10] sts.
With RS of work facing rejoin yarn to rem sts and complete to match first side, reversing shaping.

Front
Work as given for back until work measures 13[13½:14:14½]in from hemline, ending with a RS row.
Divide for front opening
Next row Patt 62[65:68:71] sts, cast off 8 sts, patt to end.
Complete left side first. Cont without shaping until work measures 18½in from hemline, ending with a WS row.
Work pocket
Next row Patt 23[26:29:32] sts, sl next 26 sts on to a holder, K up 1 st from behind each st on holder, patt to end.
Keeping patt correct cont until work measures same as back to armhole, ending at armhole edge.
Shape armhole
Cast off 4 sts at beg of next row and 3 sts at beg of foll alt row. Work 1 row. Dec one st at armhole edge on next and every alt row until 49[51:53:55] sts rem. Cont without shaping until armhole measures 4½[5:5½:6]in from beg, ending at neck edge.
Shape neck
Next row Cast off 10[11:11:12] sts, patt to end.
Dec one st at neck edge on next and foll 5 alt rows. 33[34:36:37] sts. Cont without shaping until arm-

hole measures same as back to shoulder, ending at armhole edge.

Shape shoulder
Cast off 8[8:9:9] sts at beg of next and foll 2 alt rows. Work 1 row. Cast off rem 9[10:9:10] sts.
With RS of work facing rejoin yarn to rem sts and complete to match first side, omitting pocket.

Complete pocket
Using No. 11 needles and with RS of work facing K across sts on holder, inc one st at each end. 28 sts. Beg with a P row work 2¼in st st, ending with a P row. Change to No. 13 needles.
Next row P1, *K2, P2, rep from * to last 3 sts, K2, P1.
Next row K1, *P2, K2, rep from * to last 3 sts, P2, K1.
Rep last 2 rows until rib measures ¾in. Cast off in rib.

Sleeves
Using No. 13 needles cast on 78[82:86:90] sts.
1st row K2, *P2, K2, rep from * to end.
2nd row P2, *K2, P2, rep from * to end.
Rep these 2 rows until work measures 1in from beg. Change to No. 11 needles. Cont in rib inc one st at each end of next and every foll 8th row until there are 92[96:100:104] sts. Cont without shaping until sleeve measures 6in from beg, ending with a WS row.

Shape top
Cast off 4 sts at beg of next 2 rows. Dec one st at each end of next and every alt row until 40 sts rem, ending with a WS row. Cast off at beg of next and every row 2 sts 8 times and 3 sts 4 times. Cast off rem 12 sts.

Button band
Using No. 13 needles and with RS of work facing, K up 110 sts along left front edge. Work 12 rows K2, P2 rib as given for sleeves. Cast off in rib.

Buttonhole band
Using No. 13 needles and with RS of work facing, K up 110 sts along right front edge. Work 5 rows K2, P2 rib.
Next row (buttonhole row) Rib 16 sts, (cast off 4 sts, rib 20 sts) 3 times, cast off 4 sts, rib to end.
Next row Rib to end, casting on 4 sts above those cast off in previous row.
Work 5 rows rib. Cast off in rib.

Neckband
Join shoulder seams. Using No. 13 needles and with RS of work facing, K up 154[158:162:166] sts round neck. Work 5 rows K2, P2 rib.
Next row (buttonhole row) Rib 4 sts, cast off 4 sts, rib to end.
Next row Rib to end, casting on 4 sts above those cast off in previous row.
Work 5 rows rib. Cast off in rib.

To make up
Press each piece under a damp cloth with a warm iron. Join side and sleeve seams. Set in sleeves. Sew down pocket. Press seams. Sew on buttons.

9 *Lacy blouse*

Sizes
To fit 34[36:38:40]in bust
Length to shoulder, 21[21½:22:22½]in
Sleeve seam, 17½in
The figures in brackets [] refer to the 36, 38 and 40in sizes respectively

Tension
5½ sts and 7½ rows to 1in over patt worked on No.9 needles

Materials
4[4:5:5] balls Pingouin Classic Crylor
One pair No.9 needles, one pair No.12 needles
17 buttons

Back
Using No.12 needles cast on 143[151:161:169] sts.
1st row K1, *P1, K1, rep from * to end.
2nd row P1, *K1, P1, rep from * to end.
Rep these 2 rows until work measures 1¼in from beg, ending with a 2nd row and dec one st at end of last row on 34 and 38in sizes only. 142[151:160:169] sts. Change to No.9 needles.
Next row *K1, K2 tog, rep from * to last st, K1. 95[101:107:113] sts. Commence patt.
1st row (WS) P to end.
2nd row K4, *yfwd, sl 1, K2 tog, psso, yfwd, K3, rep from * to last st, K1.
3rd row As 1st.
4th row K1, *yfwd, sl 1, K2 tog, psso, yfwd, K3, rep from * to last 4 sts, yfwd, sl 1, K2 tog, yfwd, K1.
These 4 rows form patt. Cont in patt until work measures 14in from beg, ending with a WS row.

Shape armholes
Keeping patt correct cast off 6 sts at beg of next 2 rows. Dec one st at each end of next and foll 6[7:8:9] alt rows. 69[73:77:81] sts. Cont without shaping until armholes measure 7[7½:8:8½]in from beg, ending with a WS row.

Shape shoulders
Cast off at beg of next and every row 6[7:7:7] sts 4 times and 7[6:7:8] sts twice. Cast off rem 31[33:35:37] sts.

Front
Work as given for back until work measures 9in from beg, ending with a RS row.

Divide for front opening
Next row P45[48:51:54] sts, cast off 5 sts, P to end.
Complete this side first. Cont in patt keeping one st at inside edge in g st throughout, until work measures same as back to underarm, ending with a WS row.

Shape armhole
Cast off 6 sts at beg of next row. Work 1 row. Dec one st at armhole edge on next and foll 6[7:8:9] alt rows. 32[34:36:38] sts. Cont without shaping until armhole measures 5[5½:6:6½]in from beg, ending at centre front edge.

Shape neck
Cast off at beg of next and foll alt rows 5[6:7:8] sts once and 2 sts twice. Dec one st at neck edge on foll 4 alt rows. Cont without shaping until armhole measures same as back to shoulder, ending at armhole edge.

Shape shoulder
Cast off at beg of next and every alt row 6[7:7:7] sts twice and 7[6:7:8] sts once.
With RS of work facing, rejoin yarn to rem sts and complete to match first side, reversing shaping.

Sleeves
Using No.12 needles cast on 55[61:67:73] sts. Work 4in rib as given for back, ending with a 2nd row and inc 16 sts evenly across last row. 71[77:83:89] sts. Change to No.9 needles. Cont in patt as given for back until sleeve measures 17½in from beg, ending with a WS row.

Shape top
Cast off 6 sts at beg of next 2 rows. Dec one st at each end of next and foll 11[12:13:14] alt rows. Cast off at beg of next and every row 2 sts 6[8:10:12] times and 3 sts 4 times. Cast off rem 11 sts.

Button band
Using No.12 needles cast on 15 sts. Work in rib as given for back until band measures same as front opening. Cast off in rib. Mark positions for 7 buttons, the first to come ½in below neck edge and the last to come 1in above front opening with 5 more evenly spaced between.

Buttonhole band
Work as given for button band, making buttonholes as markers are reached as foll:
Next row (buttonhole row) Rib 6 sts, cast off 3 sts, rib to end.
Next row Rib to end, casting on 3 sts above those cast off in previous row.

Collar
Using No.12 needles cast on 51[55:59:63] sts. Work 1 row rib as given for back. Cont in rib, casting on 6 sts at beg of next 10 rows. Cont without shaping until work measures 5in from beg. Cast off in rib.

To make up
Do not press. Join shoulder seams. Set in sleeves. Join side and sleeve seams, leaving cuffs open. Work a row of dc along front edge of cuff opening, making 5 buttons loops of 3 ch each evenly spaced. Sew on buttons. Sew on front bands. Sew on collar. Sew on buttons.

10 *Random striped shirt*

Sizes
To fit 34[36:38:40:42]in bust
Length to shoulder, 26½[27:27½:28:28½]in
Sleeve seam, 14[14½:15:15½:16]in
The figures in brackets [] refer to the 36, 38, 40 and 42in sizes respectively

Tension
5½ sts and 7 rows to 1in over st st worked on No.8 needles

Materials
10[11:12:13:14] balls Patons Double Knitting in main shade, A
2 balls each in contrast colours B and D
4 balls in contrast colour, C
One pair No.8 needles
One pair No.10 needles
Four buttons

Back
Using No.10 needles and A, cast on 97[103:109:115:121] sts. Beg with a K row work 1½in st st, ending with a K row.
Next row K all sts tbl to form hemline.
Change to No.8 needles. Beg with a K row, cont in st st working 2 rows B, 2 rows C, 2 rows A, 2 rows D, then cont in A until work measures 2in from hemline, ending with a P row.

Shape sides
Dec one st at each end of next and every foll 12th row until 85[91:97:103:109] sts rem, *at the same time* work striped patt, as foll: Cont in A until work measures 7¼in from hemline, **2 rows D, 2 A, 2 D, 2 A, 2 C, 2 A, 4 B, 2 A, 2 B, 2 D, 2 A, 8 C, 2 A, 4 D, **, then cont in A only until work measures 17in from hemline, ending with a P row. Work 4 rows B, 6 A.

Shape armholes
Using C, cast off 3 sts at beg of next 2 rows. 79[85:91:97:103] sts.
3rd row Using A, K1, K2 tog, K to last 3 sts, K2 tog tbl, K1.
4th row Using A, P to end.
5th and 6th rows Using B, work 2 rows without shaping.
7th and 8th rows Using A, as 3rd and 4th rows.
9th and 10th rows Using A, as 5th and 6th rows.
11th and 12th rows Using A, as 3rd and 4th rows.
13th and 14th rows Using D, as 5th and 6th rows.
15th and 16th rows Using D, as 3rd and 4th rows.
Rep 3rd and 4th rows until 27[29:31:33:35] sts rem, working 2 rows B, 2 A, 16 C, 2 D, then cont in A only, ending with a P row.
Cast off.

Front
Work as given for back until work measures 17in from beg, ending with a K row and 1 row less of stripe in A.
Divide for front opening
Next row Using A, P40[43:46:49:52] sts, cast off 5 sts, P to end.
Complete this side first. Cont in striped patt until work measures same as back to underarm, ending at armhole edge.
Shape armhole
Keeping striped patt correct, cast off 3 sts at beg of next row. Work 1 row.
Next row K1, K2 tog, K to end.
Beg with a P row work 3 rows st st.
Rep last 4 rows twice more, then cont to dec at beg of every alt row until 18[19:20:21:22] sts rem, ending at front edge.
Shape neck
Next row Cast off 4[5:6:7:8] sts, P to end.
Next row K1, K2 tog, K to last 2 sts, K2 tog.
Next row P to end.
Rep last 2 rows 4 times more. Cont to dec at armhole edge only on every alt row until 2 sts rem, ending with a K row.
Next row P2 tog. Fasten off.
With RS of work facing, rejoin yarn to rem sts and complete to match first side, reversing shaping.

Sleeves
Using No.10 needles and A, cast on 45[45:47:47:49] sts.
1st row K1, *P1, K1, rep from * to end.
2nd row P1, *K1, P1, rep from * to end.
Rep these 2 rows for 2in, ending with a 2nd row and inc 4 sts evenly across last row. 49[49:51:51:53] sts. Change to No.8 needles. Beg with a K row, cont in st st inc one st at each end of 7th and every foll 8th row until there are 69[71:73:75:77] sts, *at the same time* working in stripes as foll: Cont in A until work measures 3¼[3½:3¾:4:4¼]in, work as given for back from ** to **, then cont in A until sleeve measures 12½[13:13½:14:14½]in from beg, ending with a P row. Work 4 rows B, 6 A.
Shape top
Working in stripes to match back, cast off 3 sts at beg of next 2 rows.
Next row K1, K2 tog, K to last 3 sts, K2 tog tbl, K1.
Beg with a P row work 3 rows st st. Cont to dec on every 4th row 1[2:3:4:5] times more. 59 sts. P 1 row. Dec one st at each end of next and every alt row until 7 sts rem, ending with a P row. Cast off.

Buttonhole band
Using No.10 needles and A, cast on 55[57:61:63:67] sts. Beg with a 2nd row work 3 rows rib as given for sleeves.
Next row Rib 4[6:7:9:10] sts, *cast off 2 sts, rib 13[13:14:14:15] sts, rep from * twice more, cast off 2 sts, rib to end.
Next row Rib to end, casting on 2 sts above those cast off in previous row.
Work 3 more rows in rib. Cast off in rib.

Button band
Work as given for buttonhole band, omitting buttonholes.

Collar
Using No.10 needles and C, cast on 35[37:39:41:43] sts. Work 1 row K1, P1 rib. Cont in rib, casting on at beg of next and every row 8 sts 6 times and 10 sts 4 times. 123[125:127:129:131] sts. Cont in rib until work measures 3[3:3¼:3¼:3½]in from beg. Break off C. Join in B and K 1 row, then rib 1 row. Break off B. Join in A and K 1 row, then rib 3 rows. Cast off loosely in rib.

To make up
Press each piece under a damp cloth with a warm iron. Join raglan seams. Join side and sleeve seams. Sew on front bands. Sew on collar. Turn hem to WS at hemline and sl st down. Press all seams. Sew on buttons.

11 *Long line cardigan*

Sizes
To fit 34[36:38:40]in bust
Length to shoulder, 29[29½:30:30½]in
Sleeve seam, 17in
The figures in brackets [] refer to the 36, 38 and 40in sizes respectively
Tension
6 sts and 7 rows to 1in over st st worked on No.9 needles
Materials
16[17:18:19] balls Templetons Antler Double Crepe
One pair No.9 needles
One pair No.11 needles
Six buttons

Back
Using No.11 needles cast on 123[129:135:141] sts.
1st row K1, *P1, K1, rep from * to end.
2nd row P1, *K1, P1, rep from * to end.
Rep these 2 rows until work measures 1½in from beg, ending with a 2nd row. Change to No.9 needles. Commence patt.
1st row K34[36:37:39] sts, sl 1, K53[55:59:61] sts, sl 1, K34[36:37:39] sts.
2nd row P to end.
Rep these 2 rows 4 times more. Keeping sl st correct, dec one st at each end of next and every foll 10th row until 107[113:119:125] sts rem. Cont without shaping until work measures 13½in from beg, ending with a P row.
Next row K25[27:28:30] sts, Pl, K1, P1, K51[53:57:59] sts, P1, K1, P1, K to end.
Next row P25[27:28:30] sts, K1, P1, K1, P51[53:57:59] sts, K1, P1, K1, P to end.
Next row K23[25:26:28] sts, P1, (K1, P1) 3 times, K47[49:53:55] sts, P1, (K1, P1) 3 times, K to end.
Next row P23[25:26:28] sts, K1, (P1, K1) 3 times, P47[49:53:55] sts, K1, (P1, K1) 3 times, P to end.
Cont in this way working 2 more sts into rib at each side of each point on every alt row, until all sts are in rib. Cont in rib until work measures 22in from beg, ending with a WS row.
Shape armholes
Cast off at beg of next and every row 6 sts twice and 2[2:3:3] sts twice. Dec one st at each end of next and foll 3[4:4:5] alt rows. 83[87:91:95] sts. Cont in rib without shaping until armholes measure 7[7½:8:8½]in from beg, ending with a WS row.
Shape shoulders
Cast off at beg of next and every row 6[6:7:7] sts 6 times and 7[8:6:7] sts twice. Cast off rem 33[35:37:39] sts.

Left front
Using No.11 needles cast on 61[65:67:71] sts. Work in rib as given for back for 1½in, ending with a 2nd row and inc one st at end of last row on 34 and 38in sizes only. 62[65:68:71] sts. Change to No.9 needles.
Next row K35[37:38:40] sts, sl 1, K to end.
Next row P to end.
Rep last 2 rows 4 times more. Dec one st at beg of next and every foll 10th row until 53[56:59:62] sts rem. Cont without shaping until work measures 13½in from beg, ending with a P row.
Next row K25[27:28:30] sts, P1, K1, P1, K to end.
Next row P25[26:28:29] sts, K1, P1, K1, P to end.
Next row K23[25:26:28] sts, P1, (K1, P1) 3 times, K to end.
Cont in this way to match back until all sts are in rib. Cont without shaping until work measures same as back to underarm, ending with a WS row.
Shape armhole
Cast off at beg of next and foll alt row 6 sts once and 2[2:3:3] sts once. Dec one st at armhole edge on next and foll 3[4:4:5] alt rows. 41[43:45:47] sts. Cont without shaping until armhole measures 6[6½:7:7½]in from beg, ending at front edge.
Shape neck
Cast off 10[11:12:13] sts at beg of next row, then 2 sts at beg of foll 3 alt rows, ending at armhole edge.
Shape shoulder
Cast off at beg of next and every alt row 6[6:7:7] sts 3 times and 7[8:6:7] sts once.

Right front
Work to match left front, reversing patt and shaping.

Sleeves
Using No.11 needles cast on 47[49:51:53] sts. Work 2in rib as given for back, ending with a 2nd row. Change to No.9 needles.
Next row K3 sts, rib to last 3 sts, K3 sts.
Next row P3 sts, rib to last 3 sts, P3 sts.
Next row K5 sts, rib to last 5 sts, K5 sts.
Next row P5 sts, rib to last 5 sts, P5 sts.
Cont in this way working 2 sts more in st st at either side of rib on next and every alt row until all sts are in st st, when the centre st is sl on every K row, *at the same time* when work measures 3in from beg, inc one st at each end of next and every foll 8th row until there are 77[79:81:83] sts. Cont without shaping until sleeve measures 17in from beg, ending with a P row.
Shape top
Cast off 6 sts at beg of next 2 rows. Dec one st at each end of next and every alt row until 35 sts rem. Cast off at beg of next and every row 2 sts 8 times and 3 sts 4 times. Cast off rem 7 sts.

Collar
Join shoulder seams. Using No.11 needles and with RS of work facing, K up 81[85:89:93] sts round neck edge. Work 4½[4¾:5:5¼]in K1, P1 rib. Cast off in rib.

Left front band
Using No 11 needles cast on 235[241:247:253] sts. Work 1½in K1, P1 rib. Cast off in rib.

Right front band
Using No.11 needles cast on 235[241:247:253] sts. Work ¾in K1, P1 rib.
Next row (buttonhole row) Rib 22 sts, (cast off 4 sts, rib 18 sts) 6 times, rib to end.
Next row Rib to end, casting on 4 sts above those cast off in previous row.
Cont in rib until work measures 1½in from beg. Cast off in rib.

To make up
Do not press. Join side and sleeve seams. Set in sleeves. Sew on front bands beg at top edge of collar, with 22 sts at end of buttonhole band. Sew on buttons.

12 *Long crochet cardigan*

Sizes
To fit 34[36:38:40:42:44]in bust
Length to shoulder, 25½[26:26½:27:27½:28]in adjustable
Sleeve seam, 17½in adjustable
The figures in brackets [] refer to the 36, 38, 40, 42 and 44in sizes respectively.

Tension

8 sts and 7 rows to 2in over htr worked on No.4·50 (ISR) crochet hook

Materials

30[31:32:33:34:35] balls Sirdar Double Crepe
One No.4·50 (ISR) crochet hook
One No.5·00 (ISR) crochet hook
8 buttons

Back

Using No.4·50 (ISR) hook make 70[74:78:82:86:90] ch.

1st row Into 3rd ch from hook work 1htr, 1htr into each ch to end. Turn. 68[72:76:80:84:88] sts.
2nd row 2ch to count as first htr, 1htr into each htr to end. Turn.
The 2nd row forms patt. Cont in patt until work measures 18in from beg, or required length to underarm.

Shape armholes

Next row Ss over first 4[4:5:5:6:6] sts, 2ch, patt to last 4[4:5:5:6:6] sts, turn.
Dec one st at each end of next 4[5:5:6:6:7] rows. 52[54:56:58:60:62] sts. Cont without shaping until armholes measure 7½[8:8½:9:9½:10]in from beg.

Shape shoulders

Next row Ss over first 5 sts, 2ch, patt to last 5 sts, turn.
Rep this row once more.
Next row Ss over first 5[5:6:6:7:7] sts, 2ch, patt to last 5[5:6:6:7:7] sts.
Fasten off.

Left front

Using No.4·50 (ISR) hook make 39[41:43:45:47:49] ch. Work as given for back until work measures same as back to underarm. 37[39:41:43:45:47] sts.

Shape armhole

Next row Ss over first 4[4:5:5:6:6] sts, 2ch, patt to end.
Dec one st at armhole edge on next 4[5:5:6:6:7] rows. 29[30:31:32:33:34] sts. Cont without shaping until armhole measures 5½[6:6½:7:7½:8]in from beg, ending at armhole edge.

Shape neck

Next row Patt to last 6[7:7:8:8:9] sts, turn.
Next row Ss over first 2 sts, 2ch, patt to end.
Next row Patt to last 2 sts, turn.
Dec one st at neck edge on next 4 rows, ending at neck edge.

Shape shoulder

Next row Patt to last 5 sts, turn.
Next row Ss over first 5 sts, 2ch, patt to end.
Fasten off. Mark positions for 8 buttons, first to come ½in above lower edge and last to come ½in below neck shaping, with 6 more evenly spaced between.

Right front

Work as given for left front, reversing all shaping and making buttonholes as markers are reached, as foll:
Next row (RS) 2ch, work 2htr, 2ch, miss 2 sts, work in htr to end. Turn.
Next row Work in htr to end, working 2htr into 2ch sp. Turn.

Sleeves

Using No.5·00(ISR) hook make 36[40:40:44:44:48] ch.

1st row Into 3rd ch from hook work 1tr, 1tr into each ch to end. Turn. 34[38:38:42:42:46] tr.
2nd row 3ch, insert hook under stem of next tr from right to left on the front of work and work 1tr – called raised trF –, *insert hook under stem of next tr from right to left on the back of work and work 1tr – called raised trB–, work another raised trB, work 2 raised trF, rep from * to end. Turn.
3rd row 3ch, raised trB, *2 raised trF, 2 raised trB, rep from * to end. Turn.
The last 2 rows form patt. Cont in patt, inc one st at each end of next and every foll 6th row, working extra sts into patt, until there are 52[56:56:60:60:64] sts. Cont without shaping until sleeve measures 17½in from beg, or required length to underarm, ending with a WS row.

Shape top

Dec one st at each end of next 16[18:18:20:20:22] rows. 20 sts. Dec 2 sts at each end of next 3 rows. Fasten off.

Pockets (make 2)

Using No.5·00 (ISR) hook make 20 ch. Work first 3 rows as given for sleeves. 18 sts. Rep patt rows 7 times more, then first patt row once. Work 1 row dc, then work 2nd row dc working from left to right.
Fasten off.

Collar

Join shoulder seams. Using No.5·00(ISR) hook, miss first 2 sts at neck edge, rejoin yarn to next st, work 46[46:46:50:50:50] tr to last 2 sts from other end of neck, turn.
Work 10 rows patt as given for sleeves.
Fasten off.

To make up

Press each piece under a damp cloth with a warm iron. Set in sleeves. Join side and sleeve seams. Press seams.
Work edging Using No.4·50 (ISR) hook, beg at one side seam and work 1 row dc round all edges, then work a 2nd row dc working from left to right. Fasten off. Work round sleeve edges in same way. Sew on pockets. Press seams.
Sew on buttons.

13 Midi dress with bell sleeves

Sizes

To fit 34[36:38:40:42]in bust
36[38:40:42:44]in hips
Length to shoulder, 43[43½:44:44½:45]in
Sleeve seam, 6in
The figures in brackets [] refer to the 36, 38, 40 and 42in sizes respectively

Tension

5 sts and 2 rows to 1in over patt worked on No.4·00 (ISR) crochet hook

Materials

22[23:24:25:26] balls Emu Crochet Wool Double Knitting in main shade, A
3 balls in contrast colour, B
1 ball in contrast colour, C
One No.4·00 (ISR) crochet hook
One No.3·50 (ISR) crochet hook

Back

Using No.4·00 (ISR) hook and B, make 147[151:157:161:167] ch.

1st row Work 1tr into 5th ch from hook, *1ch, miss 1ch, 1tr into next ch, rep from * to end. Turn. 145[149:155:159:165] sts.
2nd row 4ch to count as first tr and 1ch, *work 1tr into next tr, 1ch, rep from * to end, 1tr in turning ch. Turn.
The 2nd row forms patt and is rep throughout. Work 2 more rows with B, 3 rows A, 2 rows C, 3 rows B, then 1 row A. Cont with A only, dec 2 sts at each end of next and every foll 6th row until 113[117:123:127:133] sts rem. Cont without shaping, if necessary, until work measures 25in from beg. Change to No.3·50 (ISR) hook.
Next row 3ch, 1tr in ch sp, 1tr into next tr, * miss next ch sp, 1tr into next tr, 1tr in ch sp, 1tr into next tr, rep from * to last 2[2:0:0:2] sts, 1tr in ch sp, 1tr in last tr [1tr in ch sp, 1tr in last tr:0:0:1tr in ch sp, 1tr in last tr].
86[89:93:96:101] sts.
Next row 3ch, work 1tr into each tr to end, dec one st at end of row on 32in size only, and inc one st at end of row on 38in size only. 85[89:93:97:101] sts.
Work in tr as set for 5in. Change to No.4·00 (ISR) hook. Cont in patt as at beg until work measures 36in from beg.

Shape armholes

Next row Ss over first 6 sts, 3ch, patt to last 6 sts, turn.
Next row Ss over first 2 sts, 3ch, patt to last 2 sts, turn.
Next row Patt to end.
Rep last 2 rows 1[2:2:3:3] times more. 65[65:69:69:73] sts. Cont without shaping until armholes measure 7[7½:8:8½:9]in from beg.

Shape shoulders

Next row Ss over first 6 sts, 3ch, patt to last 6 sts, turn.
Next row Ss over first 6[6:8:8:10] sts, 3ch, patt to last 6[6:8:8:10] sts.
Fasten off.

Front

Work as given for back until armhole shaping is completed. 65[65:69:69:73] sts.

Divide for opening

Next row Patt 31[31:33:33:35] sts, turn and complete this side first.
Cont until armhole measures 5[5½:6:6½:7]in from beg, ending at neck edge.

Shape neck

Next row Ss over first 15 sts, 3ch, patt to end. Turn.
Next row Patt to last 2 sts, turn.
Next row Ss over first 2 sts, 3ch, patt to end. Turn. 12[12:14:14:16] sts.
Cont without shaping until armhole measures same as back to shoulder, ending at armhole edge.

Shape shoulder

Next row Ss over first 6 sts, 3ch, patt to end. Turn.
Next row Ss over rem sts. Fasten off.
Miss 1ch, 1tr, 1ch at centre front, rejoin yarn to rem sts and patt to end. Complete to match first side, reversing shaping.

Sleeves

Using No.4·00 (ISR) hook and A, make 99[101:103:105:107] ch. Work 5 rows patt as given for back. 97[99:101:103:105] sts.
Next row 4ch, *1tr into next tr, 1ch, 1tr into next tr, 1ch, miss next ch, tr and ch, rep from * 14[15:15:15:16] times more, 1tr into next tr, patt to end. 67[67:69:71:71] sts.
Cont in patt until sleeve measures 6in from beg.

Shape top

Next row Ss over first 6 sts, 3ch, patt to last 6 sts, turn.
Next row Ss over first 2 sts, 3ch, patt to last 2 sts, turn.
Rep last row 8[8:8:9:9] times more.
Next row Ss over first 3 sts, 3ch, patt to last 3 sts, turn.
Rep last row once more.
Fasten off.

To make up

Press each piece under a damp cloth with a warm iron. Join shoulder seams. Set in sleeves. Join side and sleeve seams.
Edgings Using No.4·00 (ISR) hook, B, and with RS of work facing, work a row of dc around lower edge, working into each tr and ch sp. Do not turn work but work a 2nd row of dc from left to right to form crab edging. Work round sleeves and front opening and neck in same way. Using 3 strands of A make a ch cord and thread through holes in front opening. Using 3 strands of yarn make a ch cord in A, B and C. Thread cord in C through first row at beg of skirt, cord in A through 3rd row and cord in B through 2nd row of stripe in A.
Press all seams.

14 Jumper suit with striped bib

Sizes
To fit 34[36:38]in bust
36[38:40] hips
Jumper length to shoulder, 25[25½:26]in
Sleeve seam, 8in
Skirt length, 23in adjustable
The figures in brackets [] refer to the 36 and 38in sizes respectively

Tension
4½ sts and 5½ rows to 1in over st st worked on No.4 needles

Materials
11[12:13] balls Hayfield Croft Thickerknit in main shade, A
1[1-2] balls in contrast colour, B
One pair No.4 needles
One pair No.6 needles
Set of 4 No.6 needles pointed at both ends
Waist length of elastic
One 8in zip fastener

Jumper back
Using No.6 needles and A, cast on 88[92:96] sts. Beg with a K row work 1½in st st, ending with a K row.
Next row K all sts tbl to form hemline.
Change to No.4 needles. Beg with a K row cont in st st until work measures 14in from hemline.
Dec one st at each end of next and every foll 6th row until 80[84:88] sts rem. Cont without shaping until work measures 18in from hemline, ending with a P row.
Shape armholes
Cast off 5 sts at beg of next 2 rows. Dec one st at each end of next 3[4:5] alt rows. 64[66:68] sts. Cont without shaping until armholes measure 7[7½:8]in from beg, ending with a P row.
Shape shoulders
Cast off at beg of next and every row 5 sts 4 times and 4[5:6] sts twice.
Leave rem 36 sts on holder.

Front
Work as given for back until front measures 7in from hemline, ending with a P row.
Divide for front opening
Next row K44[46:48] sts, turn and leave rem sts on holder.
Complete this side first, shaping side edge to match back and dec one st at centre front edge on every foll 5th row until work measures same as back to underarm, ending at armhole edge.
Shape armhole
Cast off 5 sts at beg of next row. Work 1 row. Dec one st at beg of next and foll 2[3:4] alt rows. Keeping armhole edge straight, cont to dec at front edge as before until 14[15:16] sts rem. Cont without shaping until armhole measures same as back to shoulder, ending at armhole edge
Shape shoulder
Cast off at beg of next and every alt row 5 sts twice and 4[5:6] sts once.
With RS of work facing, rejoin yarn to rem sts and complete to match first side, reversing shaping.

Sleeves
Using No.6 needles and A, cast on 46[48:50] sts. Beg with a K row 1in st st, ending with a K row.
Next row K all sts tbl to form hemline.
Change to No.4 needles. Beg with a K row cont in st st, inc one st at each end of 3rd and every foll 4th row until there are 62[64:66] sts. Cont without shaping until sleeve measures 8in from hemline, ending with a P row.

Shape top
Cast off 5 sts at beg of next 2 rows. Dec one st at each end of next and every alt row until 30 sts rem. Cast off at beg of next and every row 2 sts 8 times and 3 sts twice. Cast off rem 8 sts.

Neckband
Join shoulder seams. Using set of 4 No.6 needles, B and with RS of work facing, K across sts on back neck holder, K up 72[74:76] sts down side of front neck and K up 72[74:76] sts up other side of front neck. 180[184:188] sts.
Next round K to 2 sts before centre front, sl 1, K1, psso, K2 tog, K to end.
Rep this round 5 times more, then P1 round still dec at centre front.
Next round K to 2 sts before centre front, K twice into next st, K2, K twice into next st, K to end.
Rep this round 4 times more. Cast off loosely, still inc at centre front.

Striped bib
Using No.4 needles and A, cast on 4 sts. Beg with a K row work 8 rows st st, inc one st at each end of 3rd and foll 4th row. Cont in st st, working 6 rows B, 6 rows A, and inc at each end of every foll 4th row until there are 50 sts. Cont without shaping until 5th row of 8th stripe in B has been worked. 97 rows in all. Change to No.6 needles. K 1 row. Beg with a K row, cont with B and work 5 more rows. Cast off loosely.

To make up
Press each piece under a damp cloth with a warm iron. Set in sleeves. Join side and sleeve seams. Turn all hems to WS and sl st down. Sew in striped bib to front opening. Press seams.

Skirt back
Using No. 6 needles and A, cast on 90[94:98] sts and beg at hem. Beg with a K row work 1½in st st, ending with a K row.
Next row K all sts tbl to form hemline.
Change to No.4 needles. Beg with a K row cont in st st, working (6 rows A, 6 rows B) twice. Cont in st st using A only until work measures 14in from hemline, or required length to waist less 9in, ending with a P row.
Next row K22[23:24] sts, K2 tog, K42[44:46] sts, sl 1, K1, psso, K22[23:24] sts.
Beg with a P row work 3 rows st st.
Next row K22[23:24] sts, K2 tog, K40[42:44] sts, sl 1, K1, psso, K22[23:24] sts.
Beg with a P row work 3 rows st st.
Cont dec in this way on next and every foll 4th row until 66[70:74] sts rem. Cont without shaping for further 1in, ending with a K row. Change to No.6 needles.
Next row K all sts tbl to mark fold line.
Beg with a K row cont in st st for 1in. Cast off loosely.

Skirt front
Work as given for back.

To make up
Press as given for jumper. Join side seams leaving 8in open from fold line on left side for zip. Sew in zip. Fold hem and waistband to WS and sl st down. Press seams. Thread elastic through waistband and secure at each end.

15 Striped maxi dress

Sizes
To fit 32[34:36:38:40]in bust
34[36:38:40:42]in hips
Length to shoulder, 46[47:48:49:50]in
The figures in brackets [] refer to the 34, 36, 38 and 40in sizes respectively

Tension
6 sts and 8 rows to 1in over st st worked on No.9 needles

Materials
16[18:20:22:24] balls Emu Scotch Double Knitting in main shade, A
2[2:3:3:4] balls of contrast colour, B
One pair No.9 needles
One No.3·00 (ISR) crochet hook
20 buttons

Back
Using No.9 needles and A, cast on 158[164:170:176:182] sts. Beg with a K row work 4in st st, ending with a P row.
Shape skirt
Next row K19 sts, sl 1, K1, psso, K40[42:44:46:48] sts, sl 1, K1, psso, K32[34:36:38:40] sts, K2 tog, K40[42:44:46:48] sts, K2 tog, K19 sts.
Beg with a P row cont in st st until work measures 5in from beg, then work 2 rows with B. Cont with A until 17 rows in all have been worked from last dec row.
Next row K19 sts, sl 1, K1, psso, K38[40:42:44:46] sts, sl 1, K1, psso, K32[34:36:38:40] sts, K2 tog, K38[40:42:44:46] sts, K2 tog, K19 sts.
Cont to dec in this way on every foll 18th row until 98[104:110:116:122] sts rem, *at the same time* work in stripes as foll: 4½in A, 2 rows B, 4in A, 2 rows B, 3½in A, 2 rows B, 3in A, 2 rows B, 2½in A, 2 rows B, 2in A, 2 rows B, 1½in A, 2 rows B. Complete back working in 8 rows A and 2 rows B throughout. Cont without shaping until work measures 38[38½: 39:39½:40]in from beg.
End with a P row.
Shape armholes
Cast off at beg of next and every row 8 sts twice and 2[2:3:3:4] sts twice. Dec one st at each end of next and foll 3[4:4:5:5] alt rows. 70[74:78:82:86] sts. Cont without shaping until armholes measure 7[7½:8:8½:9]in from beg, ending with a P row.
Shape neck and shoulders
Next row K19[20:21:22:23] sts, turn and leave rem sts on holder.
Next row Cast off 4 sts, P to end.
Next row Cast off 6[6:7:7:8] sts, K to end.
Next row Cast off 4 sts, P to end.
Cast off rem 5[6:6:7:7] sts.
With RS of work facing, rejoin yarn to rem sts and cast off 32[34:36:38:40] sts, K to end. P 1 row. Complete to match first side reversing shaping.

Left front
Using No.9 needles and A, cast on 79[82:85:88:91] sts. Beg with a K row work 4in st st, ending with a P row.
Shape skirt
Next row K19 sts, sl 1, K1, psso K40[42:44:46:48] sts, sl 1, K1, psso, K to end.
Cont working in striped sequence as given for back, dec in this way on every foll 18th row until 49[52:55:58:61] sts rem. Cont without shaping until work measures same as back to underarm, ending at armhole edge.
Shape armhole
Cast off at beg of next and foll alt row 8 sts once and 2[2:3:3:4] sts once. Dec one st at armhole edge on foll 4[5:5:6:6] alt rows. 35[37:39:41:43] sts. Cont without shaping until armhole measures 3[3½:4: 4½:5]in from beg, ending at front edge.
Shape neck
Cast off at beg of next and foll alt rows 9[9:10:10: 11] sts once, 5[6:6:7:7] sts once, 4 sts once and 2 sts twice. Dec one st at neck edge on foll 2 alt rows. Cont without shaping until armhole measures same as back to shoulder.
End at armhole edge.
Shape shoulder
Cast off at beg of next and foll alt row 6[6:7:7:8] sts once and 5[6:6:7:7] sts once.

Right front
Work as given for left front, reversing shaping.

To make up
Press each piece under a damp cloth with a warm iron. Join shoulder and side seams.
Armbands Using No.3·00 (ISR) hook, A and with RS of work facing, work 1 round dc round armhole. Join with a ss.
Next round 2ch, *1ch, miss 1dc, 1dc into next dc, rep from * to end. Join with ss to 2nd of first 2ch. Rep last round 4 times more. Fasten off.
Borders Mark positions for 20 buttons on left front, first to come 1½in from lower edge and last level with neck shaping with 18 spaced at equal intervals. Work round all edges as given for armbands, working 1dc, 1ch, 1dc into each corner on every row and making buttonholes on 4th row as markers are reached by working 3ch and missing 3 sts, and working 3 sts in to each 3ch sp on 5th row.
Press all seams. Sew on buttons.

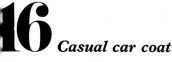

16 Casual car coat

Sizes
To fit 34[36:38:40:42]in bust
    36[38:40:42:44]in hips
Length to shoulder, 33[33½:34:34½:35]in, adjustable.
Sleeve seam, 16½[17:17:17½:18]in, adjustable
The figures in brackets [] refer to the 36, 38, 40 and 42in sizes respectively
Tension
4 sts and 5 rows to 1in over st st worked on No.5 needles
Materials
14[15:16:17:18] balls Listers Prema Bulky Knitting in main shade, A
1 ball of contrast colour, B
One pair No.5 needles
One pair No.7 needles
7 buttons

Back
Using No.7 needles and A, cast on 107[111:115:119:123] sts.
1st row K1, *P1, K1, rep from * to end.
2nd row P1, *K1, P1, rep from * to end.
Rep these 2 rows twice more. Change to No.5 needles. Beg with a K row cont in st st for 2½in, ending with a P row.
Shape darts
Next row K1, K2 tog, K19[20:21:22:23] sts, sl 1, K1, psso, K59[61:63:65:67] sts, K2 tog, K19[20:21:22:23] sts, sl 1, K1, psso, K1.
Beg with a P row work 11 rows st st.
Next row K1, K2 tog, K18[19:20:21:22] sts, sl 1, K1, psso, K57[59:61:63:65] sts, K2 tog, K18[19:20:21:22] sts, sl 1, K1, psso, K1.
Beg with a P row work 11 rows st st.
Cont dec in this way on next and every foll 12th row until 75[79:83:87:91] sts rem. Cont without shaping until work measures 25in from beg, or required length to underarm.
End with a P row.
Shape armholes
Cast off 3 sts at beg of next 2 rows.
Next row K3 sts, K2 tog, K to last 5 sts, sl 1, K1, psso, K3 sts.
Next row P to end.
Rep last 2 rows until 29[29:31:31:33] sts rem, ending with a K row. **Join in B and change to No.7 needles. P 1 row, then work 1st row of rib. Join in A. P 1 row, then rib 6 rows. Join in B. K 1 row.
Cast off loosely in rib. **

Left front
Using No.5 needles and A, cast on 23 sts for pocket lining. Beg with a K row work 4in st st, ending with a P row. Leave sts on holder. Using No.7 needles and A, cast on 53[55:57:59:61] sts. Work 6 rows rib as given for back. Change to No.5 needles. Beg with a K row cont in st st for 2½in.
End with a P row.
Shape darts
Next row K1, K2 tog, K19[20:21:22:23] sts, sl 1, K1, psso, K to end
Beg with a P row work 11 rows st st.
Next row K1, K2 tog, K18[19:20:21:22] sts, sl 1, K1, psso, K to end.
Beg with a P row work 11 rows st st.
Cont dec in this way on next and every foll 12th row until work measures 8in from beg, ending with a P row.
Place pocket
Next row K to last 33[33:34:34:35] sts, sl next 23 sts on to holder, K across pocket lining sts, K to end.
Cont to dec on every foll 12th row as before until 37[39:41:43:45] sts rem. Cont without shaping until work measures 10 rows less than back to underarm.
End with a P row.
Shape front edge
Next row K to last 3 sts, K2 tog, K1.
Beg with a P row work 5 rows st st.
Next row K to last 3 sts, K2 tog, K1.
Beg with a P row work 3 rows st st.
Shape armhole
Next row Cast off 3 sts, K to end.
Next row P to end.
Next row K3 sts, K2 tog, K to last 3 sts, K2 tog, K1.
Cont to dec at front edge on every foll 6th row 7[7:8:8:9] times more, *at the same time* dec at raglan edge on every alt row until 4 sts rem, ending with a P row.
Next row K2 sts, K2 tog.
Next row P3 sts.
Next row K1 st, K2 tog.
Next row P2 tog. Fasten off.

Right front
Work as given for left front, reversing position of pocket and all shaping.

Sleeves
Using No.7 needles and A, cast on 33[35:37:39:41] sts. Work 4in rib as given for back, ending with a 2nd row. Change to No.5 needles. Beg with a K row cont in st st, inc one st at each end of first and every foll 6th row until there are 53[57:59:63:65] sts. Cont without shaping until sleeve measures 16½[17:17:17½:18]in from beg, or required length to underarm ending with a P row. Mark each end of last row with coloured thread. Work 4 more rows.
Shape top
Next row K3 sts, K2 tog, K to last 5 sts, sl 1, K1, psso, K3 sts.
Next row P to end.
Rep last 2 rows until 7 sts rem, ending with a K row. Work as given for back from ** to **

Left front band
Using No.7 needles and A, with RS of work facing K up 125[127:129:131:133] sts along front edge. Work as given for back from ** to **.
Mark positions for 7 buttons, first to come 1½in from lower edge and last to come ½in below beg of front shaping, with 5 more evenly spaced between.

Right front band
Work as given for left front band, making buttonholes on 3rd row of rib in A as foll: Rib to first marker, (cast off 2 sts, rib to next marker) 6 times, cast off 2 sts, rib to end.
Next row Rib to end, casting on 2 sts above those cast off in previous row.

Pocket tops
Using No.7 needles and with WS of work facing, sl 23 sts from holder on to needle and work as given for back from ** to **, inc one st at each end of first row.

To make up
Press each piece under a damp cloth with a warm iron. Join raglan seams, sewing last 4 rows of sleeves to cast off sts at underarm. Join side and sleeve seams. Sew down pocket tops and pocket linings. Press all seams. Sew on buttons.

17 Casual suit

Sizes
To fit 34[36:38:40]in bust
    36[38:40:42]in hips
Jacket length to shoulder, 21[21½:22:22½]in
Sleeve seam, 16½[17:17½:18]in
Skirt length, 19½[20:20½:21]in
The figures in brackets [] refer to the 36, 38 and 40in sizes respectively
Tension
5 sts and 7 rows to 1in over rib worked on No.9 needles
Materials
18[19:21:23] balls Patons Camelot
One pair No.9 needles
One pair No.11 needles
Five buttons
Waist length of elastic
One 7in zip fastener

Jacket back
Using No.11 needles cast on 87[92:97:102] sts.
1st row P2, *K3, P2, rep from * to end.
2nd row K2, *P3, K2, rep from * to end.
These 2 rows form patt. Cont in patt until work measures 1½in from beg. Change to No.9 needles and cont in patt until work measures 14in from beg, ending with a 2nd row.
Shape armholes
Cast off 5 sts at beg of next 2 rows. Dec one st at each end of next and foll 4[5:6:7] alt rows. 67[70:73:76] sts. Cont without shaping until armholes measure 7[7½:8:8½]in from beg, ending with a WS row.
Shape shoulders
Cast off at beg of next and every row 7 sts 4 times and 5[6:7:8] sts twice. Cast off rem 29[30:31:32] sts.

Jacket left front
Using No.9 needles cast on 21 sts for pocket lining. Beg with a K row work 4in st st, ending with a K row.
Next row P3 sts, *P twice into next st, P2, rep from * to end. 27 sts. Leave sts on holder.
Using No.11 needles cast on 51[54:56:59] sts.
1st row *P2, K3, rep from * to last 11[9:11:9] sts, P2[0:2:0] sts, K4, sl 1, K4.
2nd row P9 sts, K2[0:2:0] sts, *P3, K2, rep from * to end.
Rep these 2 rows for 1½in. Change to No.9 needles and cont in patt until work measures 5in from beg, ending with a WS row.
Place pocket
Next row Rib 10 sts, sl next 27 sts on to holder for pocket top, rib across sts of pocket lining, rib to end.
Cont in patt until work measures same as back to underarm, ending with a WS row.
Shape armhole and front edge
Next row Cast off 5 sts, patt to last 11 sts, K2 tog, K4, sl 1, K4.
Next row Patt to end.
Next row K2 tog, patt to end.

Next row P9 sts, P2 tog, patt to end.
Cont dec at armhole edge on every alt row 4[5:6:7] times more, *at the same time* cont to dec at front edge on every 3rd row until 28[29:30:31] sts rem. Cont without shaping until armhole measures same as back to shoulder, ending at armhole edge.

Shape shoulder
Cast off at beg of next and every alt row 7 sts twice and 5[6:7:8] sts once. Cont on rem 9 sts until strip is long enough to reach centre back neck. Cast off.

Right front
Work pocket lining as given for left front.
Using No.11 needles cast on 51[54:56:59] sts.
1st row K4, sl 1, K4, P2[0:2:0] sts, *K3, P2, rep from * to end.
2nd row *K2, P3, rep from * to last 11[9:11:9] sts, K2[0:2:0] sts, P9.
Cont as given for left front until work measures 2½in from beg, ending with a WS row.
Next row (buttonhole row) K1, cast off 2 sts, K1, sl 1, K1, cast off 2 sts, patt to end.
Next row Patt to end, casting on 2 sts above those cast off in previous row.
Complete to match left front, reversing position of pocket and all shaping and making 4 more buttonholes in same way at intervals of 2½in from previous one.

Sleeves
Using No.11 needles cast on 32[37:37:42] sts. Work in rib as given for back for 1½in. Change to No.9 needles and cont in rib, inc one st at each end of next and every foll 6th row until there are 62[67:71:74] sts. Cont without shaping until sleeve measures 16½[17:17½:18]in from beg, ending with a WS row.

Shape top
Cast off 5 sts at beg of next 2 rows. Dec one st at each end of next and foll 6[8:10:11] alt rows. Cast off at beg of next and every row 2 sts 8 times and 3 sts 4 times. Cast off rem 10[11:11:12] sts.

Pocket tops
Using No.11 needles and with RS of work facing, work across pocket top sts, as foll: K3 sts, *K2 tog, K2, rep from * to end. 21 sts. Beg with a P row work 4 rows st st.
Next row K all sts tbl to mark fold line.
Beg with a K row work 4 rows st st. Cast off.

To make up
Do not press. Join shoulder seams. Set in sleeves. Join side and sleeve seams. Join ends of front band. Fold front bands in half to WS and sl st down and sew to back neck. Neaten buttonholes. Sew down pocket tops and pocket linings. Sew on buttons.

Skirt back
Using No.11 needles cast on 66[70:74:78] sts and beg at waist.
1st row K2, *P2, K2, rep from * to end.
2nd row P2, *K2, P2, rep from * to end.
Rep these 2 rows for 1¼in, ending with a 2nd row. Change to No.9 needles. Beg with a K row cont in st st for 4 rows.
Shape darts
Next row K21[22:23:24] sts, K twice into next st, K24[26:26:28] sts, K twice into next st, K21[22:23: 24] sts.
Beg with a P row work 3 rows st st.
Next row K21[22:23:24] sts, K twice into next st, K24[26:28:30] sts, K twice into next st, K21[22:23: 24] sts.
Beg with a P row work 3 rows st st.
Cont to inc in this way on next and every foll 4th row until there are 96[100:104:108] sts, then on every foll 8th row until work measures 19½[20:20½: 21]in from beg, ending with a K row. Change to No.11 needles.
Next row K all sts tbl to form hemline.
Beg with a K row work 1½in st st. Cast off loosely.

Skirt front
Work as given for back.

To make up
Do not press. Join side seams leaving 7in open at top of left seam for zip. Sew in zip. Sew elastic inside waist edge with casing st. Turn hem to WS and sl st down.

18 *Crochet cardigan (for larger ladies too)*

Sizes
As given for jersey (design 19)
Length to shoulder, 20½[21:21½:22:22½]in
Sleeve seam, 16[16½:17:17½:18]in
Tension
As given for jersey
Materials
14[16:18:20:21] balls Wendy Tricel/Nylon 4 ply Crepe in main shade, A
2[3:3:4:4] balls in contrast colour, B
One No.3·50 (ISR) crochet hook
One No.3·00 (ISR) crochet hook
7 buttons

Back
Using No.3·50 (ISR) hook and A, make 114[126: 138:150:162] ch. Work in patt as given for jersey back. 28[31:34:37:40] gr. Cont in patt until work measures 11½in from beg, or required length to underarm.
Shape armholes
Work as given for jersey back. 22[23:24:25:26] gr. Cont without shaping until armholes measure 8½[9: 9½:10:10½]in from beg. Fasten off.

Left front
Using No.3·50 (ISR) hook and A, make 54[62:66: 74:78] ch. Work in patt as given for back. 13[15:16: 18:19] gr. Cont in patt until work measures same as back to underarm.
Shape armhole
Next row Ss over first 1[1:2:2:3] gr, patt to end. Turn.
Next row Patt to last gr, turn.
Next row Ss over first gr, patt to end. Turn.
Cont to dec 1 gr at armhole edge in this way until 10[11:11:12:12] gr rem. Cont without shaping until armhole measures 4½[5:5½:6:6½]in from beg, ending at armhole edge.
Shape neck
Work as given for jersey front. Fasten off.

Right front
Work as given for left front, reversing shaping.

Sleeves
Using No.3·50 (ISR) hook and A, make 50[54:58: 62:66] ch. Work in patt as given for back. 12[13:14: 15:16] gr. Cont in patt until work measures 2[2¼:2½: 2¾:3]in from beg.
Shape sleeve
1st row 3ch, work 2tr, 3ch, 1dc into first loop, patt to end. Turn.
2nd row 3ch, work 2tr, 3ch, 1dc into first loop, patt to end, ending with 2tr in turning ch. Turn.
3rd row As 2nd.
4th row 3ch, work 2tr, 3ch, 1dc into first loop, patt to end, ending with 2tr, 3ch, 1dc in turning ch. Turn.
5th row Patt to end, ending with 2tr, 3ch, 1dc in turning ch. Turn. 1 gr inc at each end.
6th, 7th and 8th rows Work in patt.
Rep last 8 rows 3 times more. 20[21:22:23:24] gr. Cont without shaping until sleeve measures 16[16½: 17:17½:18]in from beg. Work a further 2[2:4:4:6] rows.

Shape top
Work as given for jersey.

Edging
Join shoulder and side seams. Work edging as given for jersey round front edges, neck and lower edges. Work in same way round sleeves.

To make up
Press as given for jersey. Join sleeve seams leaving last 2[2:4:4:6] rows open. Set in sleeves, sewing open part to first dec row of armholes of back and front. Press seams. Sew on buttons, using holes in border patt as buttonholes.

19 *Crochet jersey (for larger ladies too)*

Sizes
To fit 32/34[36/38:40/42:44/46:48/50]in bust
Length to shoulder, 19½[20:20½:21:21½]in
Sleeve seam, 2½[2¾:3:3¼:3½]in
The figures in brackets [] refer to the 36/38, 40/42, 44/46 and 48/50in sizes respectively
Tension
3 gr and 5 rows to 2in over patt worked on No.3·50 (ISR) crochet hook
Materials
10[12:13:15:16] balls Wendy Tricel/Nylon 4 ply Crepe in main shade, A
1[1:2:2:2] balls of contrast colour, B
One No.3·50 (ISR) crochet hook
One No.3·00(ISR) crochet hook

Back
Using No.3·50 (ISR) hook and A, make 106[118: 130:142:154] ch.
1st row Into 5th ch from hook work 1tr, 3ch, 1dc, *miss 3ch, work 2tr, 3ch, 1dc into next ch, rep from * to last st, 1tr in last ch. Turn.
2nd row 2ch, work 2tr, 3ch, 1dc into each 3ch loop to end, ending with 1tr in turning ch. Turn. 26[29: 32:35:38] gr.
The 2nd row forms patt. Cont in patt until work measures 11in from beg, or required length to underarm.
Shape armholes
Next row Ss over first 1[1:2:2:3] gr, patt to last 1[1:2:2:3] gr, turn.
Next row Ss over first gr, patt to last gr, turn.
Rep last row 1[2:2:3:3] times more. 20[21:22:23: 24] gr.
Cont without shaping until armholes measure 8[8½:9:9½:10]in from beg. Fasten off.

Front
Work as given for back until armhole shaping is completed. Cont without shaping until armholes measure 4[4½:5:5½:6]in from beg.
Shape neck
Next row Patt over first 6[6:7:7:8] gr, turn and leave rem sts.
Cont on these sts until armhole measures same as back to shoulder. Fasten off.
Miss 8[9:8:9:8] gr in centre, rejoin yarn to rem 6[6:7:7:8] gr and patt to end. Complete to match first side.

Sleeves
Using No.3·50 (ISR) hook and A, make 78[82:86: 90:94] ch. Work in patt as given for back. 19[20:21: 22:23] gr. Cont in patt until work measures 2[2¼: 2½:2¾:3]in from beg. Work a further 2[2:4:4:6] rows.
Shape top
Dec 1 gr at beg of next 10[10:12:12:14] rows, then at each end of next 2[3:2:3:2] rows.
Fasten off.

Edging

Join right shoulder seam. Using No.3·00 (ISR) hook and B, rejoin yarn at neck edge and work 1dc, then work 3tr, 3ch, 1dc into each 3ch loop or into turning ch of every alt row right round neck. Break off B. Using No.3·00 (ISR) hook and A, return to beg of last row, rejoin yarn and work 1dc, *2ch, 1dc in 3ch loop of gr, 1ch, 1dc between gr, rep from * ending with 1dc in last st, turn.
Next row 1ch, work 1dc, 3ch, 1dc into each 2ch loop to end, ending with 1dc in last st. Fasten off. Work edging round sleeves and lower edge in same way.

To make up

Press each piece under a damp cloth with a cool iron. Join left shoulder seam. Set in sleeves, sewing the last 2[2:4:4:6] rows of sleeve seams to first dec row at armholes of back and front. Join side and sleeve seams. Press seams.

20 Crochet jacket and beret

Sizes
To fit a 34/36in bust
Length to shoulder, 22in
Sleeve seam, 18in
Tension
Each square motif measures 2¼in by 2¼in worked on No.3·00 (ISR) crochet hook
Materials
Jacket 12 balls Robin Tricel/Nylon Perle 4 ply
Beret 2 balls
One No.3·00 (ISR) crochet hook

Jacket

Square motif Using No. 3·00 (ISR) hook make 6ch. Join with a ss into first ch to form circle.
1st round 4ch, (1tr into circle, 1ch) 7 times. Join with a ss to 3rd of first 4ch.
2nd round 4ch, work 3dtr into first ch sp keeping last loop of each st on hook, yrh and draw through all loops on hook, (4ch, work 4dtr into next ch sp keeping last loop of each st on hook, yrh and draw through all loops on hook) 7 times, 4ch. Join with a ss to 3rd of first 4ch.
3rd round (3ch, 1tr in 4ch loop at corner, 3ch, 1dc in top of next dtr gr, 4ch, 1dc in top of next dtr gr) 4 times, working last dc into base of first 3ch. Fasten off.
Make 265 more squares in same way.

Gore
Using No.3·00 (ISR) hook make 6ch. Join with a ss into first ch to form circle.
1st round As 1st round of square.
2nd round 4ch, gr of 3dtr in first ch sp, (4ch, gr of 4dtr in next ch sp) 3 times, turn.
3rd round 3ch, 1tr in 4ch loop, 3ch, 1dc in top of next gr, 4ch, 1dc in top of next gr, 3ch, 1tr in 4ch loop, 4ch, 1dc in top of next gr – this is the lower edge and 2 corners of the gore –, cont round work with 4ch, (gr of 3tr instead of dtr in next ch sp, 3ch) into each of next 4 one ch sp, 4ch. Join with a ss to top of next dtr gr, turn.
4th round 5ch, 1tr in loop between first 2 tr gr, (3ch, 1tr in next loop) twice, 5ch, 1dc in top of first dtr gr, turn.
5th round 4ch, 1dc in first loop, 3ch, 1tr in next loop, 3ch, 1tr in next tr, 3ch, 1tr in next loop, 3ch, 1dc in next loop, 4ch. Join with a ss to top of dtr gr, turn.
6th round Ss along to dc, 5ch, miss 1 loop, 1dc in next loop, 4ch, 1tr in next tr, 4ch, 1dc in loop, 5ch, miss next loop. Join with ss into dc. Fasten off.
Work 1 more gore in same way.

To make up

Join squares as shown in diagrams for body and sleeves. Join 2 squares at front shoulder to first 2 squares at each back shoulder, leaving 3 squares for back neck. Sew the 6 squares at top of sleeves into armholes, 3 to back armhole and 3 to front armhole. Sew bottom edge of gore to the square at underarm, then sew the sides of the gore to the top part of sleeve seam.
Join rem of sleeve seam.
Edging Using No.3·00 (ISR) hook and with RS of work facing, beg at bottom of right front edge, work in dc along first 7 squares ending with 1dc in tr at corner of 7th square, then work across corner with 3ch, gr of 4dtr in 4ch loop, 3ch, gr of 4dtr in 4ch loop at side of next square, 3ch, 1dc in tr at corner, work across next corner in same way, cont in dc round neck, working in same way across corners, then cont round left side of neck working across corners, and down left front edge and round lower edge. Fasten off. Work a row of dc round sleeve edges. Press work lightly under a damp cloth with a cool iron.

Beret

Make 43 square motifs as given for jacket but working 1st and 2nd rounds only.

To make up

Join squares as shown in diagram for beret, then join the outside squares thus forming a beret shape.
Edging Using No.3·00 (ISR) hook and with RS of work facing, work round edge, working 1dc into each loop in the squares and working 2ch and 3ch between dc alternately. Work 4 more rounds dc, working 3dc into each ch loop. Fasten off.

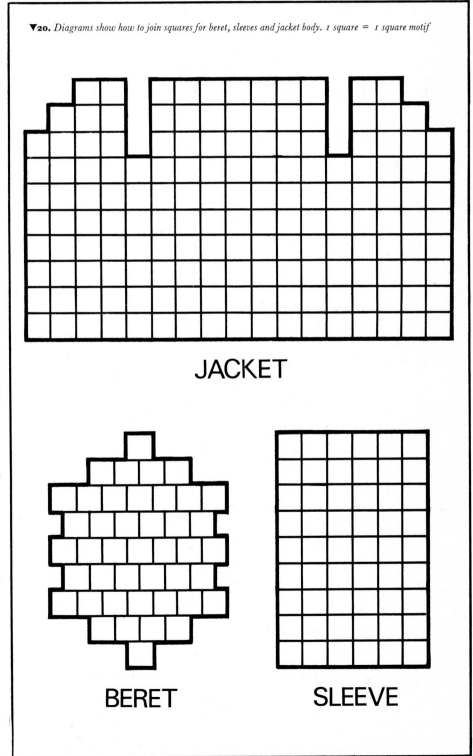

▼20. *Diagrams show how to join squares for beret, sleeves and jacket body.* 1 square = 1 square motif

JACKET

BERET   SLEEVE

21 Sleeveless crochet dress

Sizes
To fit 34[37:40]in bust
36[39:42]in hips
The figures in brackets [] refer to the 37 and 40in sizes respectively
Length to shoulder, 36[37:38]in

Gauge
5 loops and 10 rows to 4in over patt worked on No.D crochet hook

Materials
13[14:16] balls Coats & Clarks' O.N.T. "Speed Cro-Sheen"
No.D crochet hook

Back
Using No.D crochet hook ch 95[103:111].
1st row Into 5th ch from hook work 1dc, ch3, 1dc into same st, *skip ch3, work 1dc, ch3, 1dc all into next ch, rep from * ending with ch1, skip ch1, 1dc in last ch. Turn. 23[25:27] loops.
2nd row Ch3, work 5dc into each ch3 loop, ending with 1dc in turning ch. Turn.
3rd row *Work 1dc, ch3, 1dc all into 3rd of 5dc gr on previous row, rep from * ending with 1dc in turning ch. Turn.
The 2nd and 3rd rows form patt. Cont in patt until work measures 29[29½:30]in from beg, ending with a 3rd row.
Shape armholes
Next row Ss over first 2 loops, ch3, patt to last 2 loops, 1dc in sp before next loop, turn.
Next row Patt to end.
Next row Ss over first loop, ch3, patt to last loop, 1dc in sp before next loop, turn. 17[19:21] loops.
Cont without shaping until armholes measure 4½[5:5½]in from beg, ending with a 3rd row.
Shape neck
Next row Patt over 4[4:5] loops, turn and leave rem sts unworked.
Cont in patt until armhole measures 7[7½:8]in from beg, ending with a 3rd row. Fasten off. Skip first 9[11:11] loops, attach yarn to rem sts and patt over last 4[4:5] loops.
Complete to correspond to first side.

Front
Work as given for back.

Belt
Using No.D crochet hook make a ch approx 54in long. Work 1 row sc along ch. Fasten off.

Finishing
Press each piece under a damp cloth with a warm iron. Join shoulder and side seams. Work 2 rounds of sc around neck and armhole edges. Work 2 rounds sc around lower edge working 3sc into each loop and 1sc between 2dc of first row. Press seams.

22 Crochet jacket

Sizes
To fit 34[37:40]in bust
The figures in brackets [] refer to the 37 and 40in sizes respectively
Length to shoulder, 21[22:23]in
Sleeve seam, 13[13½:14]in

Gauge
As given for dress (design 21)

Materials
10[11:12] balls Coats & Clarks' O.N.T. "Speed Cro-Sheen"
No.D crochet hook

Back
Work as given for dress back (No. 21) until work measures 14[14½:15]in from beg, ending with a 3rd row.
Shape armholes
Next row Ss over first 2 loops, ch3, patt to last 2 loops, 1dc in sp before next loop, turn.
Next row Patt to end.
Next row Ss over first loop, ch3, patt to last loop, 1dc in sp before next loop, turn.
Cont in patt until armholes measure 7[7½:8]in from beg, ending with a 3rd row.
Shape neck and shoulders
Next row Patt over first 5[5:6] loops, turn and work 1 more row on these sts. Fasten off.
Skip 7[9:9] loops in center, attach yarn to rem sts and patt over last 5[5:6] loops, turn and work 1 more row. Fasten off.

Left front
Using No.D crochet hook ch 47[51:55].
Work in patt as given for back (No. 21). 11[12:13] loops. Cont in patt until work measures same as back to underarm, ending with a 3rd row.
Shape armhole
Next row Ss over first 2 loops, ch3, patt to end. Turn.
Next row Patt to end. Turn.
Next row Ss over first loop, ch3, patt to end. Turn. 8[9:10] loops.
Cont without shaping until armhole measures 4½[5:5½]in from beg, ending at armhole edge.
Shape neck
Next row Patt to last 2 loops, 1dc in sp before next loop, turn.
Next row Patt to end. Turn.
Next row Patt to last loop, 1dc in sp before last loop, turn.
Rep last 2 rows 0[1:1] times more. Cont without shaping until armhole measures same as back to shoulder, ending with a 3rd row. Fasten off.

Right front
Work as given for left front, reversing all shaping.

Sleeves
Using No.D crochet hook ch 47[51:55].
Work 9 rows patt.
Next row Ch3, 2dc in same place, work 5dc in each loop to end, 3dc in turning ch. Turn.
Next row Ch3, 1dc on next 2dc, work 1dc, ch3, 1dc all into 3rd of next 5dc gr, patt to end, ending with 2dc, then 1dc in turning ch. Turn.
Next row Ch3, 2dc in each of next 2dc, work 5dc in each loop, ending with 2dc in each of last 2dc, 1dc in turning ch. Turn.
Next row Ch3, work 1dc, ch3, 1dc all into 2nd dc, patt to last 5dc, work 1dc, ch3, 1dc all into 3rd dc, 1dc in turning ch. Turn. (1 loop inc at each side).
Work 2 rows without shaping.
Rep last 6 rows more. 17[18:19] loops. Cont without shaping until sleeve measures 13[13½:14]in from beg, ending with a 3rd row.
Shape cap
Dec 2 loops at each end of next row. Work 3 rows without shaping. Dec one loop at each end of next and foll 4th row, then dec one loop each end every other row 3[4:4] times. 5[4:5] loops.
Fasten off.

Finishing
Press as given for dress (No. 21). Join shoulder seams. Sew in sleeves. Join side and sleeve seams. Work 2 rows sc around lower edge and sleeves as given for dress hem. Work 1 row sc up right front, around neck and down left front, turn and work 2 patt rows around these edges.
Fasten off. Press seams.

23 Granny square Cardigan

Size
To fit 34/36in bust
Length to shoulder, 24in
Sleeve seam, 16in

Gauge
Each square measures 4in by 4in worked on No. H crochet hook

Materials
5 balls Reynolds Cashmere Lamb in main color, A
3 balls each of contrast colors B and C
No.H crochet hook

Granny square motif
Using No.H crochet hook and B, ch5. Join with a ss to first ch to form circle.
1st round Using B work ch3, 2dc into circle, (3dc into circle, ch2) 3 times. Join with a ss to 3rd of first ch3.
Break off B.
2nd round Using C, join with a ss to a ch2 sp, ch3, work 2dc, ch2, 3dc into this sp, *ch2, work 3dc, ch2, 3dc into next sp, rep from * twice more, ch2. Join with a ss to 3rd of first ch3.
Break off C.
3rd round Using B, join with a ss to a ch2 sp at one corner, ch3, work 2dc, ch2, 3dc into this sp, *ch2, 3dc into next sp, ch2, work 3dc, ch2, 3dc into next sp, rep from * twice more, ch2, 3dc into next sp, ch2. Join with a ss to 3rd of first ch3.
Break off B.
4th round Using A, join with a ss to a ch2 sp at one corner, ch3, work 2dc, ch2, 3dc into this sp, *(ch2, 3dc into next sp) twice, ch2, work 3dc, ch2, 3dc into next sp, rep from * twice more, (ch2, 3dc into next sp) twice, ch2. Join with a ss to 3rd of first ch3.
Fasten off. Make 67 more squares in this manner, varying color sequence, B and C as desired but always using A for 4th round.

Half square motif
Using No.H crochet hook and B, ch5. Join with a ss to first ch to form circle.
1st round Using B work ch3, 2dc into circle, (ch2, 3dc into circle) twice. Break off B.
2nd round Using C, join with a ss to 3rd of first ch3, ch3, work 3dc, ch2, 3dc into first sp, ch2, work 3dc, ch2, 3dc into 2nd sp, ch2, 1dc in last dc. Break off C.
3rd round Using B, join with a ss to 3rd of first ch3, ch3, 1dc in first sp, ch2, work 3dc, ch2, 3dc in next sp, ch2, 3dc in next sp, ch2, work 3dc, ch2, 3dc in next sp, ch2, 2dc in next sp. Break off B.
4th round Using A, join with a ss to 3rd of first ch3, ch5, 3dc in first sp, ch2, work 3dc, ch2, 3dc in next sp, (ch2, 3dc in next sp) twice, ch2, work 3dc, ch2, 3dc in next sp, ch3, 3dc in next sp, ch2, 1dc in last dc.
Fasten off.
Make 2nd half square in same manner, using same colors.

Finishing
Press each square under a damp cloth with a warm iron. Join squares as in diagram. Using No.H crochet hook and A, work 5 rounds sc around all edges, except sleeves.
Press.

23. *Join the squares as shown, noting that the two half-squares are shown shaded. Fold along the dotted (ie shoulder) line, and join side and sleeve seams, folding the two squares at underarm in half on the dotted lines* ▶

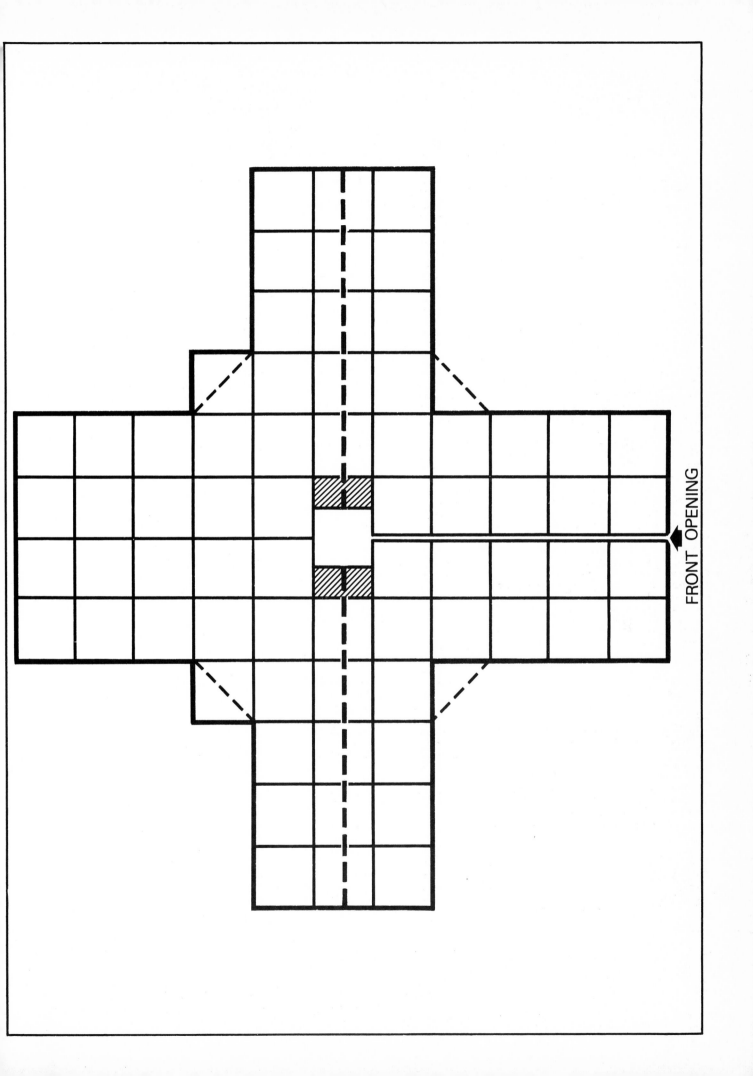

FRONT OPENING

24 Striped slip-on

Sizes
To fit 32[34:36:38]in bust
Length to shoulder, 18½[19:19½:20]in
The figures in brackets [] refer to the 34, 36 and 38in sizes respectively
Tension
7½ sts and 10 rows to 1in over st st worked on No.11 needles
Materials
4[4:5:5] balls Sirdar Fontein Crepe 4 ply in main shade, A
2 balls each of contrast colours, B, C and D
1 ball each of contrast colours, E, F and G
One pair No.11 needles
One pair No.13 needles
Set of 4 No.13 needles pointed at both ends

Back
Using No.13 needles and A, cast on 121[129:137:145] sts.
1st row K1, *P1, K1, rep from * to end.
2nd row P1, *K1, P1, rep from * to end.
Rep these 2 rows for 2½in, ending with a 2nd row. Change to No.11 needles. Beg with a P row work 2 rows reversed st st. Cont in reversed st st, working in stripes, as foll: **2 rows B, 2 rows C, 2 rows D, 2 rows A, 2 rows E, 2 rows B, 2 rows A, 2 rows F, 2 rows C, 2 rows D, 2 rows A, 2 rows G and 2 rows A. ** Rep from ** to ** until work measures 11in from beg, ending with a K row.
Shape armholes
Keeping striped sequence correct, cast off at beg of next and every row 8[9:10:11] sts twice and 4 sts twice. Dec one st at each end of next and foll 9[10:11:12] alt rows. 77[81:85:89] sts. Cont without shaping until armholes measure 7½[8:8½:9]in from beg, ending with a K row.
Shape shoulders
Cast off at beg of next and every row 6[6:7:7] sts twice and 5[6:6:7] sts twice. Leave rem 55[57:59:61] sts on holder.

Front
Work as given for back until front measures same as back to underarm.
End with a K row.
Shape armholes and neck
Cast off at beg of next and every row 8[9:10:11] sts twice and 4 sts twice.
Next row P2 tog, P32[34:36:38] sts, turn and leave rem sts on holder.
Next row Cast off 2 sts, K to end.
Next row P2 tog, P to end.
Rep last 2 rows once more, then first of them again. Dec one st at each end of next and foll 6 alt rows, then cont to dec at armhole edge only 0[1:2:3] times more. 11[12:13:14] sts. Cont without shaping until armhole measures same as back to shoulder, ending at armhole edge.
Shape shoulder
Cast off at beg of next and foll alt row 6[6:7:7] sts once and 5[6:6:7] sts once.
With RS of work facing, sl first 29[31:33:35] sts on holder and leave for centre neck, rejoin yarn to rem sts, P to last 2 sts, P2 tog. Complete to match first side, reversing shaping.

Neckband
Join shoulder seams. Using set of 4 No.13 needles, A and with RS of work facing, K across back neck sts, K up 68[71:74:77] sts down side of front neck, K across front neck sts and K up 68[71:74:77] sts up other side of neck. 220[230:240:250] sts. Work 5 rounds K1, P1 rib.
Cast off in rib.

Armbands
Using No.13 needles, A and with RS of work facing, K up 135[143:151:159] sts round armhole. Beg with a 2nd row work 5 rows rib as given for back. Cast off in rib.

To make up
Press each piece under a damp cloth with a warm iron. Join side seams. Press seams.

25 Slip-on with red lips motif

Sizes
To fit 32[34:36]in bust
Length to shoulder 18½[19½:20½]in
The figures in brackets [] refer to the 34 and 36in sizes respectively
Tension
6¼ sts and 8 rows to 1in over st st worked on No.9 needles
Materials
5[5:6] balls Patons Ninepin in main shade, black
4[4:5] balls in contrast colour, green
1[1:1] ball in contrast colour, red
One pair No.9 needles
One pair No.11 needles

Back
Using No.11 needles and black, cast on 102[106:114] sts.
1st row K2, *P2, K2, rep from * to end.
2nd row P2, *K2, P2, rep from * to end.
Rep these 2 rows for 1½in, ending with a 2nd row and dec one st in centre of last row on 32 and 36in sizes, and inc one st in centre of last row on 34in size. 101[107:113] sts. Change to No.9 needles.
** Beg with a K row work 70[74:78] rows st st. Break off black and join in green. Work 10 more rows st st.
Shape armholes
Cast off at beg of next and every row 6 sts twice, 4 sts twice and 3 sts twice. Dec one st at each end of next and foll 1[2:3] alt rows. 71[75:79] sts. Cont without shaping until armholes measure 7[7½:8]in from beg, ending with a P row.
Shape shoulders
Cast off at beg of next and every row 4 sts 4 times and 4[5:6] sts twice. Leave rem 47[49:51] sts on holder.

Front
Work as given for back until 54[58:62] rows of st st have been worked.
Next row Using first ball of black K39[42:45] sts, using red K23 sts, using 2nd ball of black K to end.
Next row P38[41:44] sts black, P25 red, P38[41:44] sts black.
Cont working in this way from chart A until 16 rows have been completed. Break off black and join in green. Work 10 more rows patt.
Shape armholes
Keeping patt correct, shape armholes as given for back.
Cont without shaping until 9 rows have been worked in green after completion of patt, ending with a P row.
Shape neck
Next row K21[22:23] sts, turn and leave rem sts on holder.
Dec one st at neck edge on every alt row until 12[13:14] sts rem. Cont without shaping until armhole measures same as back to shoulder, ending at armhole edge.
Shape shoulder
Cast off at beg of next and foll alt rows 4 sts twice and 4[5:6] sts once.
With RS of work facing, sl first 29[31:33] sts on to holder and leave for centre neck, rejoin yarn to rem sts and K to end. Complete to match first side, reversing shaping.

Neckband
Join right shoulder seam. Using No.11 needles, green and with RS of work facing, K up 49 sts down side of neck, K across sts on front neck holder, K up 49 sts up other side of neck and K across sts on back neck holder. 174[178:182] sts. Beg with a 2nd row work 7 rows rib as given for back. Cast off in rib.

Armbands
Join left shoulder seam. Using No.11 needles, green and with RS of work facing, K up 118[122:126] sts round armhole. Work as given for neckband.

To make up
Press each piece under a damp cloth with a warm iron. Join side seams. Press seams.

26 Slip-on with black star motif

Sizes
As given for Slip-on with red lips motif
Tension
As given for Slip-on with red lips motif
Materials
7[7:8] balls Patons Ninepin in main shade, yellow
2[2:3] balls in contrast colour, black
One pair No.9 needles
One pair No.11 needles

Back
Cast on and work as given for Slip-on with red lips motif to **.
Beg with a K row cont in st st, working (10 rows yellow, 10 rows black) 3 times. *** Work 20[24:28] rows yellow.
Shape armholes
Using yellow, shape armholes as given for back of Slip-on with red lips motif. 71[75:79] sts. Cont without shaping until 36[40:44] rows have been worked in yellow, then cont in stripes of 10 rows black and 10 rows yellow until armholes measure 7[7½:8]in from beg, ending with a P row.
Shape shoulders
As given for back of Slip-on with red lips motif.

Front
Work as given for back to ***. Work 2[4:6] rows yellow.
Next row Using first ball of yellow K36[39:42] sts, using black K2, using yellow K25, using black K2, using 2nd ball of yellow K to end.
Next row Using yellow P36[39:42] sts, P4 black, P21 yellow, P4 black, P to end using yellow.
Cont working in this way from chart B until 18[20:22] rows have been completed.
Shape armholes
Keeping patt correct, shape armholes as given for back. Cont without shaping until 34[38:42] rows have been worked from beg of yellow stripe, ending with a P row.
Shape neck
Next row K21[22:23] sts, turn and leave rem sts on holder.
Next row P to end.
Cont in stripes of 10 rows black and 10 rows yellow as given for back, dec one st at neck edge on next and every alt row until 12[13:14] sts rem. Cont without shaping until armhole measures same as back to shoulder, ending at armhole edge.
Shape shoulder
Cast off at beg of next and every alt row 4 sts twice

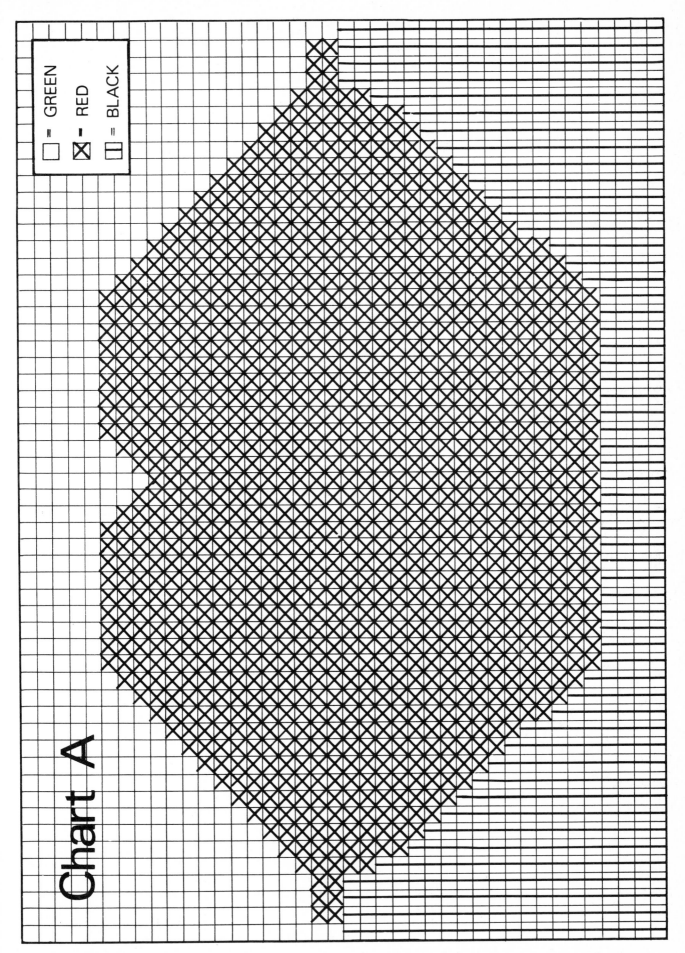

▲**25.** *The chart for the Red Lips motif indicates the part to be worked in red with X's. Each square on the chart represents one stitch*

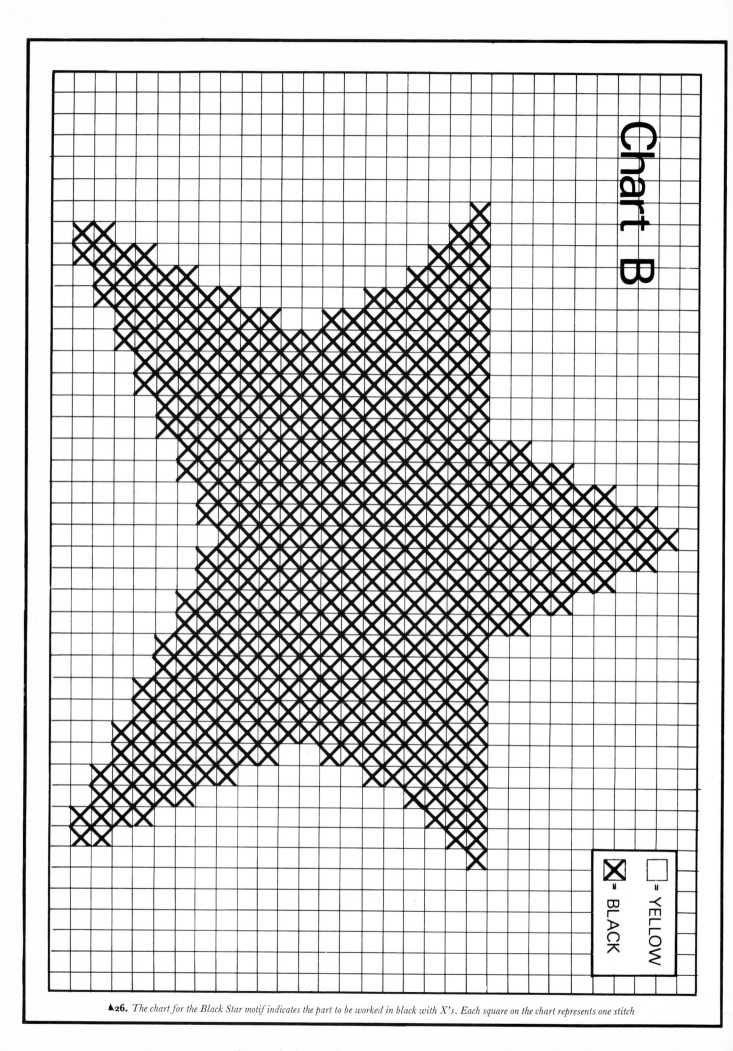

Chart B

□ = YELLOW
☒ = BLACK

▲26. *The chart for the Black Star motif indicates the part to be worked in black with X's. Each square on the chart represents one stitch*

and 4[5:6] sts once.
With RS of work facing, sl first 29[31:33] sts on holder and leave for centre neck, rejoin yarn to rem sts and K to end. Complete to match first side, reversing shaping.

Neckband and armbands
Work as given for Slip-on with red lips motif.

To make up
As given for Slip-on with red lips motif.

Lace panelled jerkin and plain skirt

Sizes
To fit 34[36:38:40:42]in bust
36[38:40:42:44]in hips
Jerkin length to shoulder, 22½[23:23½:24:24½]in adjustable
Skirt length, 20[20½:21:21½:22]in adjustable
The figures in brackets [] refer to the 36, 38, 40 and 42in sizes respectively
Tension
5 sts and 7 rows to 1in over st st worked on No.8 needles
Materials
10[11:12:13:14] balls Mahony Killowen Extra Double Knitting
One pair No.8 needles
One pair No.9 needles
Set of 4 No.9 needles pointed at both ends
Waist length of elastic
One 7in zip fastener

Jerkin back
Using No.9 needles cast on 90[94:98:102:110] sts.
1st row K2, *P2, K2, rep from * to end.
2nd row P2, *K2, P2, rep from * to end.
Rep these 2 rows until work measures 2in from beg, ending with a 2nd row and dec one st at end of last row on 34, 36 and 42in sizes, and inc one st at end of last row on 38 and 40in sizes. 89[93:99:103:109] sts.
Change to No.8 needles. Commence patt.
1st row K11[12:14:15:17] sts, *yfwd, K6, sl 1, K2 tog, psso, K6, yfwd, K11[12:13:14:15] sts, rep from * once more, yfwd, K6, sl 1, K2 tog, psso, K6, yfwd, K11[12:14:15:17] sts.
2nd and every alt row P to end.
3rd row K12[13:15:16:18] sts, *yfwd, K5, sl 1, K2 tog, psso, K5, yfwd, K13[14:15:16:17] sts, rep from * once more, yfwd, K5, sl 1, K2 tog, psso, K5, yfwd, K to end.
5th row K13[14:16:17:19] sts, *yfwd, K4, sl 1, K2 tog, psso, K4, yfwd, K15[16:17:18:19] sts, rep from * once more, yfwd, K4, sl 1, K2 tog, psso, K4, yfwd, K to end.
7th row K14[15:17:18:20] sts, *yfwd, K3, sl 1, K2 tog, psso, K3, yfwd, K17[18:19:20:21] sts, rep from * once more, yfwd, K3, sl 1, K2 tog, psso, K3, yfwd, K to end.
9th row K15[16:18:19:21] sts, *yfwd, K2, sl 1, K2 tog, psso, K2, yfwd, K19[20:21:22:23] sts, rep from * once more, yfwd, K2, sl 1, K2 tog, psso, K2, yfwd, K to end.
11th row K16[17:19:20:22] sts, *yfwd, K1, sl 1, K2 tog, psso, K1, yfwd, K21[22:23:24:25] sts, rep from * once more, yfwd, K1, sl 1, K2 tog, psso, K1, yfwd, K to end.
13th row K17[18:20:21:23] sts, *yfwd, sl 1, K2 tog, psso, yfwd, K23[24:25:26:27] sts, rep from * once more, yfwd, sl 1, K2 tog, psso, yfwd, K to end.
14th row P to end.
These 14 rows form patt. Cont in patt until work measures 14½in from beg, or required length to underarm ending with a P row.

Shape armholes
Cast off at beg of next and every row 3[3:4:4:4] sts twice, 3[3:3:3:4] sts twice and 3 sts twice. 71[75:79:83:87] sts. Cont without shaping until armholes measure 8[8½:9:9½:10]in from beg, ending with a P row.
Shape shoulders
Cast off at beg of next and every row 5[5:6:6:6] sts 6 times and 6[7:5:6:7] sts twice. Leave rem 29[31:33:35:37] sts on holder.

Jerkin front
Work as given for back until work measures 1½in less than back to underarm, ending with a P row.
Divide for neck
Next row Patt 44[46:49:51:54] sts, turn and leave rem sts on holder.
Next row P to end.
Next row Patt to last 3 sts, K2 tog, K1.
Cont to dec at neck edge in this way on every foll 4th row until work measures same as back to underarm, ending at armhole edge.
Shape armhole
Cont dec at neck edge as before, cast off at beg of next and foll alt rows 3[3:4:4:4] sts once, 3[3:3:3:4] sts once and 3 sts once. Cont to dec at neck edge on every 4th row until 21[22:23:24:25] sts rem. Cont without shaping until armhole measures same as back to shoulder, ending at armhole edge.
Shape shoulder
Cast off 5[5:6:6:6] sts at beg of next and foll 2 alt rows. Work 1 row. Cast off rem 6[7:5:6:7] sts.
With RS of work facing, leave first st on holder, rejoin yarn to rem sts and patt to end.
Next row P to end.
Next row K1, sl 1, K1, psso, patt to end.
Complete to match first side, reversing shaping.

Neckband
Join shoulder seams. Using set of 4 No.9 needles and with RS of work facing, K across sts of back neck holder, K up 70[73:76:79:82] sts down front neck, K centre front neck st and K up 71[74:77:80:83] sts up other side of front neck. 171[179:187:195:203] sts.
Next round P0[0:1:0:0], K1[2:2:0:1], (P2,K2) 24[25:26:28:29] times, P2 tog, K1, P2 tog, (K2, P2) 17[18:18:19:20] times, K1[0:2:2:1], P0[0:1:0:0].
Work 4 more rounds in rib as set, P2 tog at each side of centre st on every round. Cast off in rib still dec at centre front.

Armbands
Using No.9 needles and with RS of work facing, K up 122[126:130:134:138] sts round armhole. Beg with a 2nd row, work 5 rows rib as given for back. Cast off in rib.

To make up
Press each piece under a damp cloth with a warm iron. Join side seams. Press seams.

Skirt back
Using No.9 needles cast on 64[68:74:78:84] sts and beg at waist. Beg with a K row work 1½in st st. ending with a K row.
Next row K all sts tbl to mark foldline.
Change to No.8 needles. Beg with a K row cont in st st until work measures 2in from foldline, ending with a P row.
Shape darts
Next row K21[22:24:26:28] sts, pick up loop lying between sts and K tbl – called inc 1 –, K1, K1, K20[22:24:24:26] sts, inc 1, K1, inc 1, K21[22:24:26:28] sts.
Beg with a P row work 7 rows st st.
Next row K22[23:25:27:29] sts, inc 1, K1, inc 1, K22[24:26:26:28] sts, inc 1, K1, inc 1, K22[23:25:27:29] sts.
Beg with a P row work 7 rows st st.
Cont inc in this way on next and every foll 8th row

until there are 96[100:106:110:116] sts. Cont without shaping until work measures 20[20½:21:21½:22]in from foldline, or required length from waist, ending with a K row.
Next row K all sts tbl to mark hemline.
Change to No.9 needles. Beg with a K row work 1½in st st. Cast off loosely.

Skirt front
Work as given for back.

To make up
Press as given for jerkin. Join side seams, leaving 7in from foldline open on left seam for zip. Turn waistband and hem to WS and sl st down. Press seams. Thread elastic through waistband and secure. Sew in zip.

Bikini and long jacket

Sizes
To fit 32[35:38]in bust
34[37:40]in hips
Jacket length to shoulder, 43[44:45]in
The figures in brackets [] refer to the 35 and 38in sizes respectively
Tension
21 sts and 12 rows to 4in over tr worked on No.2·50 (ISR) crochet hook
Materials
Bikini 6[7:7] balls Twilley's Crysette
Jacket 20[22:24] balls
One No.2·50 (ISR) crochet hook
One No.2·00 (ISR) crochet hook
Reel of shirring elastic
One hook and eye
12 buttons

Bikini top
Using No.2·50 (ISR) hook make 133[137:141] ch.
1st row Into 4th ch from hook work 1tr, 1tr into each of next 46[47:48] ch, work 3tr into next ch – called tr 2 –, 1tr into each of next 16[17:18] ch, 3ch, miss 1ch, 1dc in next ch, 3ch, miss 1ch, 1tr into each of next 16[17:18] ch, inc 2, 1tr into each of next 48[49:50] ch. Turn.
2nd row Ss over first 5 sts, 3ch to count as next tr, work 43[44:45] tr, inc 2, work 17[18:19] tr, 4ch, miss (3ch, 1dc, 3ch), work 17[18:19] tr, inc 2, work 44[45:46] tr, turn.
3rd row Ss over first 5 sts, 3ch, work 39[40:41] tr, inc 2, work 18[19:20] tr, 3ch, work 1dc into 4ch loop, 3ch – called V –, work 18[19:20] tr, inc 2, work 40[41:42] tr, turn.
4th row Ss over first 5 sts, 3ch, work 35[36:37] tr, inc 2, work 19[20:21] tr, 4ch, miss V, work 19[20:21] tr, inc 2, work 36[37:38] tr, turn.
5th row Ss over first 4 sts, 3ch, work 32[33:34] tr, inc 2, work 20[21:22] tr, work V, work 20[21:22] tr, inc 2, work 33[34:35] tr, turn.
6th row Ss over first 4 sts, 3ch, work 29[30:31] tr, inc 2, work 21[22:23] tr, 4ch, miss V, work 21[22:23] tr, inc 2, work 30[31:32] tr, turn.
7th row Ss over first 4 sts, 3ch, work 49[27:28] tr, 0[inc 2:inc 2], work 0[23:24] tr, turn. 50[54:56] tr.
8th row Ss over first 2 sts, 3ch, work in tr to last 4 sts, turn.
9th row Ss over first 4[4:2] sts, 3ch, work in tr to last 2tr, turn. 38[42:46] tr.
10th row Ss over first 2tr, 3ch, work in tr to last 2tr, turn.
Rep 10th row 8[9:10] times more. 2tr. Fasten off.
Return to where work was left on 7th row, miss 4ch in centre, rejoin yarn to next st, 3ch to count as first tr, on 32in size only work in tr to last 4tr, turn, and on 35 and 38in sizes work 22[23] tr, inc 2, work in tr to last 4tr, turn.

Complete to match first side, reversing shaping.

Edging
Using No.2·00 (ISR) hook and with WS of work facing, rejoin yarn to point at top and work edging for front part between shoulder straps, as foll: *4ch, 1dc into next row, rep from * to centre, work V into centre, 1dc in next st, then work up other side in same way, ending with 1dc at top, turn.

Next row 1ch, work (2dc, 2ch, 2dc) into each 4ch loop to centre, 4ch, miss V, then work up other side in same way, ending with 1dc at top. Do not fasten off but cont with rest of edging and shoulder straps, as foll: Using No.2·00 (ISR) hook and with RS of work facing, ss down other side of point working approx 62[64:66] sts, then cont round lower edge and up other side to point, turn.

Next row (WS) Make 68[72:76] ch for shoulder strap, miss first ch, work 1dc into each of rem 67[71: 75] ch, cont in dc down side of point to back, make 20[22:24] ch for strap to fasten, turn work and miss first ch, work 1dc into each of rem 19[20:21] ch, then cont in dc round lower edge and up point to top, make 68[72:76] ch for other shoulder strap, turn and miss first ch, work 1dc into each rem 67[71:75] ch. Fasten off.

Next row Using No.2·00 (ISR) hook and with WS of work facing, rejoin yarn to inside edge of left shoulder strap and work in dc from left to right – called crab st –, round strap, round work to other strap and round strap. Fasten off.

To make up
Press work under a damp cloth with a warm iron. Sew on hook and eye to back to fasten. If required, thread shirring elastic through all edges.

Bikini pants back
Using No.2·50 (ISR) hook make 16[18:20] ch.
1st row Into 2nd ch from hook work 1dc, 1dc into each ch to end. Turn. 15[17:19] dc.
2nd row 3ch to count as first tr, work 1tr into each st to end. Turn.
3rd row 3ch, inc 2, work in tr to last 2 sts, inc 2, work 1tr. Turn.
Rep 3rd row until there are 91[97:103] tr. Turn. Break off yarn.

Shape seat
1st row Miss 12[13:14] tr, rejoin yarn to next tr, 2ch, work in tr to last 13[14:15] sts, work 1dc in next st, turn. Break off yarn.
Rep this row twice more, working 24[26:28] sts less each time, Break off yarn.
4th row Rejoin yarn at beg of row, 3ch, work in tr to end. Turn.
**5th row 3ch, work 3[6:5] tr, *3ch, miss next st, 1dc in next st, 3ch, miss next st, work 5 tr, rep from * 9[9:10] times more, 3ch, miss next st, 1dc in next st, 3ch, miss next st, work 4[7:6] tr. Turn.
6th row 3ch, work 3[6:5] tr, *4ch, miss V, work 5tr, rep from * 9[9:10] times more, 4ch, miss V, work 4[7:6] tr. Turn.
7th row 3ch, work 3[6:5] tr, *work V, work 5tr, rep from * 9[9:10] times more, work V, work 4[7:6] tr. Turn.
Rep 6th and 7th rows once more, then 6th row once. Fasten off. **

Bikini pants front
Using No.2·50 (ISR) hook make 16[18:20] ch and work 1st row as given for back. 15[17:19] dc. Work 5 rows in tr.
Next row 3ch to count as first tr, work 2tr in next tr – called inc 1 –, work in tr to last 2 sts, inc 1, 1tr in turning ch. Turn.
Rep last rows 7 times more, then inc 2 as given for back at each end of next 6[7:8] rows. Turn. Break off yarn. Make 16ch, work tr into first st of last row, inc 2, patt to last 2 sts, inc 2, work 1tr, make 19ch. Turn.
Next row Into 3rd ch from hook work 1tr, 1tr into each of next 15ch, patt across work and across 16ch. Turn. 91[97:103] sts. Work as given for back from ** to **. Fasten off.

Edging
Join 7 rows for side seams. Using No.2·00 (ISR) hook and with RS of work facing, ss round leg working one ss into each st and 2ss into each row end, turn and work 1 row dc, turn and with RS of work facing work 1 row of crab st. Work 1 row dc and 1 row crab st round top edge. Join gusset seam. Press under a damp cloth with a warm iron. If required thread shirring elastic through all edges.

Jacket back
Using No.2·50 (ISR) hook make 161[169:177] ch.
1st row (RS) Into 3rd ch from hook work 1tr, work 1tr into each ch to end. Turn. 159[167:175] tr.
2nd row 3ch to count as first tr, 1tr in next tr, *3ch, miss 1tr, 1dc in next tr, 3ch, miss 1tr, 1tr in next tr – called V –, rep from * ending with 1tr in turning ch. Turn. 39[41:43] V patt.
3rd row 3ch, 1tr in next tr, *4ch, miss V, 1tr in next tr – called 1 bar –, rep from * ending with 1tr in turning ch. Turn.
4th row 3ch, 1tr in next tr, *3ch, 1dc in bar, 3ch, 1tr in tr – also called V –, rep from * ending with 1tr in turning ch. Turn.
5th row As 3rd.
6th row 3ch, 1tr in next tr, work 10[11:12] V, 3tr in bar, 1tr in next tr – called gr –, 3 V, 1 gr, 9 V, 1 gr, 3 V, 1 gr, 10[11:12] V, 1tr in turning ch. Turn.
7th row 3ch, 1tr in next tr, work 10[11:12] bars, (1tr in each of next 4tr – also called gr), 3 bars, 1 gr, 9 bars, 1 gr, 3 bars, 1 gr, 10[11:12] bars, 1tr in turning ch. Turn.
8th row 3ch, 1tr in next tr, work 10[11:12] V, 2 gr, 1 V, 2 gr, 9 V, 2 gr, 1 V, 2 gr, 10[11:12] V, 1tr in turning ch. Turn.
Cont in patt from chart, working 1[5:5] more rows.
Next row 3ch, 1tr in next tr, work 2ch, 1dc, 2ch in next bar, patt to last bar, work 2ch, 1dc, 2ch in last bar, 1tr in turning ch. Turn.
Next row 3ch, 1tr in next tr, 2ch, 1tr in next tr, patt to last V, 2ch, 1tr in next tr, 1tr in turning ch. Turn.
Next row 3ch, 1tr in next tr, miss bar, 1tr in next tr, patt to last bar, miss bar, 1tr in next tr, 1tr in turning ch. Turn.
Next row 3ch, 1tr into sp between 2tr, patt to last 3 sts, 1tr into sp between 2tr, 1tr in turning ch. Turn. 1 V dec at each end.
Keeping patt correct throughout, (work 8 rows without shaping, then rep 4 dec rows) 6 times. 7 V dec at each side. Cont without shaping until work measures 36[36½:37]in from beg, ending with a RS row.

Shape armholes
Next row Ss over first 2 bars, patt to last 2 bars, turn.
Next row Ss over 1 bar, patt to last bar, turn.

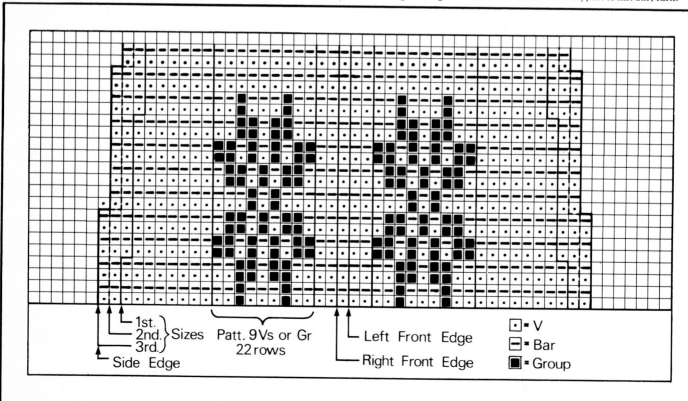

1st.
2nd. } Sizes
3rd.
Side Edge
Patt. 9 Vs or Gr
22 rows
Left Front Edge
Right Front Edge

⊡ = V
⊟ = Bar
■ = Group

Next row 3ch, 1tr in next tr, work 2ch, 1dc, 2ch in next bar, patt to last 2 bars, work 2ch, 1dc, 2ch in next bar, 1 V, 1tr in turning ch. Turn.

Next row 3ch, 1tr in next tr, 1 bar, 2ch, 1tr in next tr, patt to last 2 V, 2ch, 1tr in next tr, 1 bar, 1tr in turning ch. Turn.

Next row 3ch, 1tr in next tr, 1 V, miss bar, 1tr in next tr, patt to last 2 bars, miss next bar, 1tr in next tr, 1 V, 1tr in turning ch. Turn.

Next row 3ch, 1tr in next tr, 1 bar, working the tr into sp between 2tr, patt to last bar, working last tr into sp between 2tr, 1 bar, 1tr in turning ch. Turn.

Rep these last 4 rows 1[2:2] times more. Cont without shaping until armholes measure 7[7½:8]in from beg, ending with a RS row.

Shape neck and shoulders

Next row Mark 5[5:7] bars in centre and leave for back neck, patt to neck sts, turn.

Next row Patt to end. Turn.

Next row Ss over first bar, patt to last bar, turn.

Next row Patt to end. Turn.

Rep last 2 rows once more. Fasten off.

Miss 5[5:7] bars in centre, rejoin yarn to rem sts and complete to match first side.

Jacket right front

Using No.2·50 (ISR) hook make 81[85:89] ch. Work first 5 rows as given for back. 19[20:21] V patts.

6th row 3ch to count as first tr, 1tr in next tr, work 10[11:12] V, 1 gr, 3 V, 1 gr, 4 V, ending with 1tr in turning ch. Turn.

7th row 3ch, 1tr in next tr, 4 bars, 1 gr, 3 bars, 1 gr, work 10[11:12] bars, ending with 1tr in turning ch. Turn.

8th row 3ch, 1tr in next tr, work 10[11:12] V, 2 gr, 1 V, 2 gr, 4 V, ending with 1tr in turning ch. Turn. Cont in patt, dec at side edge as given for back, beg on 10th[14th:14th] row, until 7 V have been dec. Cont without shaping until work measures 34[34½: 35]in from beg, ending with a RS row.

Shape front edge

Dec inside 1 V as given for back armhole, and rep 4 dec rows until work measures same as back to underarm, ending at armhole edge.

Shape armhole

Still dec at front edge, shape armhole as given for back. Cont to dec at front edge only until 4[4:5] V have been dec at this edge. Cont without shaping until armhole measures same as back to shoulder, ending at armhole edge.

Shape shoulder

Next row Ss over first bar, patt to end. Turn.

Next row Patt to end. Turn.

Rep these 2 rows once more. Fasten off.

Jacket left front

Work as given for right front, reversing patt and all shaping.

To make up

Press each piece under a damp cloth with a warm iron. Join shoulder and side seams.

Front border Using No.2·00 (ISR) hook and with RS of work facing, beg at lower edge of right front and work 2dc into each row end up right front, work 44dc round neck, then 2dc into each row end down left front. Turn.

Mark positions for 12 buttons on left front, first to come ½in below beg of front shaping and last 3in from lower edge, with 10 more evenly spaced between.

Next row Work in dc to end, dec one st at each side of back neck, and making buttonholes as markers are reached on right front by working (2ch, missing 2dc, work in dc to next marker) 11 times, 2ch, miss 2dc, work in dc to end. Turn.

Next row Work in dc to end, dec one st at each side of back neck and working 2dc into each 2ch buttonhole of previous row. Do not turn.

Next row With RS of work facing work in crab st to end. Fasten off.

Armbands Using No.2·00 (ISR) hook and with RS of work facing, work 3 rows dc around armholes, then with RS of work facing work 1 row crab st. Fasten off.

Press seams and borders. Sew on buttons.

29 Bikini and short jacket

Sizes

To fit 32[34:36]in bust
34[36:38]in hips
Jacket length to shoulder, 26[27:28]in
The figures in brackets [] refer to the 34 and 36in sizes respectively

Tension

23 sts and 18 rows to 4in over htr worked on No.2·50 (ISR) crochet hook

Materials

Bikini 5[5:6] balls Wendy Invitation Crochet Cotton
Jacket 12[13:14] balls
One No.3·00 (ISR) crochet hook
One No.2·50 (ISR) crochet hook
Three small buttons
Reel shirring elastic

Bikini top

Using No.2·50 (ISR) hook make 42[46:50] ch.
1st row Into 2nd ch from hook work 1htr, 1htr into each ch to end. Turn. 41[45:49] sts.
2nd row 2ch to count as first htr, yrh, insert hook into next st and pull through loop, insert hook into next st and pull through loop, yrh and draw through all 4 loops on hook – called dec 1 –, work 17[19:21] htr, work 3htr into next st – called inc 2 –, work 17[19:21] htr, dec 1, 1htr in turning ch. Turn.
3rd row 2ch, work in htr to last 3 sts, dec 1, 1htr in turning ch. Turn.
4th row 2ch, dec 1, work 17[19:21] htr, inc 2, work 16[18:20] htr, dec 1, 1htr in turning ch. Turn.
5th row As 3rd.
6th row 2ch, dec 1, work 17[19:21] htr, inc 2, work 15[17:19] htr, dec 1, 1htr in turning ch. Turn.
7th row As 3rd.
8th row 2ch, dec 1, work 17[19:21] htr, inc 2, work 14[16:18] htr, dec 1, 1htr in turning ch. Turn.
9th row As 3rd.
10th row 2ch, dec 1, work 17[19:21] htr, inc 2, work 13[15:17] htr, dec 1, 1 htr in turning ch. Turn.
11th row As 3rd.
12th row 2ch, dec 1, work 30[34:38] htr, dec 1, 1htr in turning ch. Turn.
13th row As 3rd.
14th row 2ch, dec 1, work 27[31:35] htr, dec 1, 1htr in turning ch. Turn.
15th row As 3rd.
16th row 2ch, dec 1, work 11[13:15] htr, (dec 1) twice, work 9[11:13] htr, dec 1, 1htr in turning ch. Turn.
17th row As 3rd.
18th row 2ch, dec 1, work 8[10:12] htr, (dec 1) twice, work 7[9:11] htr, dec 1, 1htr in turning ch. Turn.
19th row As 3rd.
20th row 2ch, dec 1, work 5[7:9] htr, (dec 1) twice, work 5[7:9] htr, dec, 1htr in turning ch. Turn.
21st row 2ch, dec 1, work in htr to last 3 sts, dec 1, 1htr in turning ch. Turn.
Cont to dec in centre of row 0[1:2] times more, *at the same time* cont to dec at each end of every row until 6 sts rem.
Next row 2ch, (dec 1) twice, 1htr in turning ch. Turn.

Next row 2ch, dec 1, 1htr in turning ch. Turn.
Next row 2ch, dec 1, make 40[44:48] ch for shoulder strap, turn.
Next row (1tr, 3ch, 1tr) into 4th ch and every foll 4th ch, then cont in same way down front edge which is the edge dec on every row, working into every 3rd row, turn.
Next row (RS) Work (1dc, 3tr, 1dc) into every 3ch loop up front edge and along shoulder strap, then along other side of shoulder strap, then work in dc down other edge. Fasten off.
Make second piece in same way, reversing shaping.

Join cups

Using No.2·50 (ISR) hook make 41[45:49] ch, work 41[45:49] htr along lower edge of cup, 3dc along picot edging, miss edging of 2nd cup, work 41[45:49] htr along edge, then make 42[46:50] ch. Turn.
Next row Beg in 2nd ch from hook and work in htr along ch, lower edge and ch at other end, working over length of shirring elastic. Work a 2nd row of htr over shirring elastic, then at end of row make 3ch and ss to end of strap to make loop for button, turn and work 3dc over the 3ch loop. Fasten off.

To make up

Press lightly under a damp cloth with a warm iron. Sew button to end of strap at back and to end of one shoulder strap, using the hole in other strap to fasten.

Bikini pants back

Using No.2·50 (ISR) hook make 16[18:20] ch.
1st row Into 2nd ch from hook work 1htr, 1htr into each ch to end. Turn. 15[17:19] sts.
2nd row 3ch, insert hook into first of these 3ch and make 2htr, work in htr to last st, 2htr in last st. Turn. 3 sts inc.
Rep 2nd row 21[23:25] times more. 81[89:97] sts.
Next row 5ch, work htr into 3rd of these 5ch and rem 2ch, work in htr to end of row. Turn.
Rep last row once more. Work 9[11:13] rows without shaping. Fasten off.

Bikini pants front

Beg at cast on edge of back and work 1htr into each st. Turn. 15[17:19] sts. Work 6 rows in htr. Inc one st by working 2htr into st at each end of next and foll 2[3:3] alt rows, then at each end of next 8[8:10] rows. 37[41:47] sts. Break off yarn.
Next row Make 28[29:29] ch for leg, work over 37[41:47] sts of front, make 29[30:30] ch, turn.
Next row Into 2nd ch from hook work 1htr, 1htr into each st to end. Turn. 93[99:105] sts. Work 9[11:13] rows htr. Fasten off.

To make up

Press as given for top. Join side seams. Using No.2·50 (ISR) hook and with RS of work facing, work 1 row dc round top edge working over shirring elastic. Turn.
Next row 6ch, work 1tr into first st, *miss 3 sts, work 1tr, 3ch, 1tr into next st, rep from * to end. Join with a ss to 3rd of first 6ch. Turn.
Next row Work 1dc, 3tr, 1dc into every 3ch loop to end. Fasten off.
Using No.2·50 (ISR) hook and with RS of work facing work 1 row dc around each leg working over shirring elastic. Fasten off.

Jacket back

Using No.3·00 (ISR) hook make 102[110:118] ch.
1st row Into 2nd ch from hook work 1dc, *2ch, miss 1ch, 1dc into each of next 3ch, rep from * to last 3ch, 2ch, miss 1ch, 1dc into each of next 2ch. Turn.
2nd row 3ch, *work 1tr, 3ch, 1tr into 2ch sp, rep from * ending with 1tr in turning ch. Turn.
3rd row 3ch, *work 3dc into 3ch loop, 2ch, rep from * ending with 1dc in turning ch. Turn.

4th row 5ch, 1tr into first 2ch sp, *work 1tr, 3ch, 1tr into next 2ch sp, rep from * ending with 1tr in last 2ch sp, 2ch, 1tr in turning ch. Turn.
5th row 1ch, 1dc into first 2ch loop, *2ch, work 3dc into 3ch loop, rep from * ending with 2ch, 2dc into last 2ch loop. Turn.
Rep 2nd to 5th rows until work measures 19[19½: 20]in from beg, ending with a 3rd row. Break off yarn.

Shape armholes
Rejoin yarn to third 2ch sp, work 3ch, work 1tr, 3ch, 1tr into each 2ch sp to last three 2ch sp, 1tr in next 2ch sp, turn.
Next row As 5th patt row. 3 gr dec each end.
Cont in patt without shaping until armholes measure 7[7½:8]in from beg, ending with a 2nd or 4th row.

Shape neck
Next row Patt over 5 gr, turn and patt to end. Break off yarn.
Rejoin yarn to 5th gr from other end and work to match first side.

Jacket left front
Using No.3·00 (ISR) hook make 50[54:58] ch.
Work in patt as given for back until front measures same as back to underarm, ending with a 3rd row. Break off yarn.

Shape armhole
Rejoin yarn to third 2ch sp, work 3ch, work 1tr, 3ch, 1tr into each 2ch sp to end. Turn.
Cont without shaping until armhole measures 5[5½:6]in from beg, ending with a 2nd patt row. Break off yarn.

Shape neck
Rejoin yarn to 4th[5th:6th] loop, 3ch, patt to end. Turn. Cont without shaping until armhole measures same as back to shoulder. Fasten off.

Jacket right front
Work as given for left front, reversing all shaping.

To make up
Press as given for bikini. Join shoulder and side seams. Using No.2·50 (ISR) hook and with RS of work facing, work 1 row dc around armholes. Using No.2·50(ISR) hook and with RS of work facing work in dc up front edge as far as back neck. Break off yarn. Rejoin yarn at other side of back neck and cont in dc down left front. Break off yarn. Beg at right side seam, work 1tr, 3ch, 1tr into each loop along lower edge, into every 4th st up front edge, into each loop across back neck and into every 4th st down left front, then into each loop along lower edge to right side seam. Work 1dc, 3tr, 1dc into each 3ch loop all round edges. Fasten off. Press seams and edging. Sew on button to left neck, using hole in patt at opposite corner to fasten.

30 Crochet hat and bag

Size
Hat to fit an average head
Tension
4 sts and 2 rows to 1in over tr worked on No.5·00 (ISR) crochet hook
Materials
Hat 5 hanks Atlas Raffene in main shade, A
4 hanks in contrast colour, B
Bag 6 hanks in main shade, A
5 hanks in contrast colour, B
One No.5·00 (ISR) crochet hook
One No.4·50 (ISR) crochet hook
6in diameter ring for base of bag

Hat
Using No.5·00 (ISR) hook and A, make 5ch. Join with a ss to first ch to form circle.

1st round Using A work 2ch to count as first tr, work 21tr into circle. Using B join with a ss to 2nd of first 2ch. 22tr.
2nd round Using B work 3ch to count as first tr and 1ch, *work 1tr into next tr, 1ch, rep from * to end. Using A join with a ss to 2nd of first 3ch. 22tr.
3rd round Using A work 2ch, 1tr into same ch, * work 2tr into next ch sp, rep from * to end. Using B join with a ss to 2nd of first 2ch. 44tr.
4th round Using B work 3ch, *miss 2tr, work 1tr into next sp between tr, 1ch, rep from * to end. Using A join with a ss to 2nd of first 3ch. 29tr.
5th round Using A work 2ch, 1tr into same ch, *work 2tr into next ch sp, rep from * to end. Using B join with a ss to 2nd of first 2ch. 58tr.
6th round Using B work 3ch, *miss 1tr, work 1tr into next sp between tr, 1ch, miss 2tr, work 1tr into next sp between tr, 1ch, miss 2tr, work 1tr into next sp between tr, 1ch, rep from * to end. Using A join with a ss to 2nd of first 3ch. 35tr.
7th round As 5th.
8th round As 6th.
9th round As 5th.
10th round Using B work 3ch, *miss 2tr, work 1tr into sp between next tr, 1ch, rep from * to end. Using A join with a ss to 2nd of first 3ch.
11th round As 5th.
12th round As 10th.
13th round As 5th.
14th round As 10th.
15th round As 5th, working only 1tr into each of last 2ch. 82tr.
16th round As 10th.
17th round Using A work 2ch, 1tr into same ch, *work 3tr into next ch sp, work 2tr into next ch sp, rep from * ending with 2tr into last ch sp. Using B join with a ss in 2nd of first 2ch. 102tr.
18th round As 10th. 51tr.
19th round Using A work 2ch, 2tr into same ch, *work 3tr into next ch sp, rep from * to end. Using B join with a ss in 2nd of first 2ch. 153tr.
20th round As 10th, missing 1tr instead of 2 at end of round. 77tr.
21st round As 5th.
22nd round As 10th.
Change to No.4·50 (ISR) hook.
23rd round Using A work 2ch, work 1tr into same ch until 2 loops rem on hook, using B complete tr and make 2 more tr into same ch, using A make 2tr in next ch sp, cont in this way working alternately 4tr and 2tr into ch, changing colours after 2tr.
24th round Work alternately 2tr in A above B and 2tr in B above A.
25th round Work alternately 2dc in A above B and 2dc in B above A. Make 2ss at end of round. Fasten off.

Bag
Using No.4·50 (ISR) hook and A, make 5ch. Join with a ss to first ch to form circle. Work first 3 rounds as given for hat. 44tr.
4th round Using B work 3ch, miss 2tr, work 1tr into next tp between tr, *2ch, miss 2tr, work 1tr into next sp between tr, 1ch, miss 2tr, work 1tr into next between tr, rep from * to end. Using A join with a ss to 2nd of first 3ch. 22tr.
5th round Using A work 2ch, work 1tr into same ch, *work 3tr into next ch sp, work 2tr into next ch sp, rep from * to end. Using B join with a ss into 2nd of first 2ch. 55tr.
Change to No.5·00 (ISR) hook.
6th round Take a ring with a diameter of 6in, using B attach ring by making 1dc into each tr, inc 1dc into each 3rd tr. When 2 loops of last dc rem on hook, change colours. 74dc.
7th round Using A work in tr to end, inc 12 sts evenly in round by working 2tr into one st. Using B join with a ss. 86tr.
8th round Using B work 3ch, *miss 2tr, work 1tr into next sp between tr, 1ch, rep from * to end.

Using A join with a ss into 2nd of first 3ch. 43tr.
9th round As 3rd.
10th round As 4th.
11th round Using A work 2ch, work 1tr into same ch, *work 3tr in next ch sp, work 2tr in next ch sp, rep from * ending with 3tr in last ch sp. Using B join with a ss in 2nd of first 2ch. 108tr.
12th round Using B work 3ch, *miss 2tr, work 1tr in next sp between tr, 1ch, rep from * to end. Using A join with a ss in 2nd of first 3ch. 54tr.
13th round Using A work 2ch, work 1tr in same ch, *work 2tr in next ch sp, rep from * to end. Using B join with a ss to 2nd of first 2ch. 108tr.
14th round As 12th.
15th round As 13th.
16th round As 12th.
17th round As 11th.
18th round As 12th.
19th round As 13th.
20th round As 12th.
21st round As 13th.
22nd round As 12th.
23rd round As 11th.
24th round As 12th.
25th round As 13th.
26th round As 12th.
Change to No.4·50 (ISR) hook.
27th round As 23rd round of hat.
28th round As 24th round of hat.
29th round As 25th round of hat.

Handles
Using No.5·00 (ISR) hook and 3 strands of A, work in ch until handle is 8in long. Attach handle to side having 28tr between each end. Using No.5·00 (ISR) hook and 2 strands of B, join with a ss to where handle is attached and work 3dc, then cont working in dc all round handle. Join with a ss at other end. Work another handle in same way.

31 Sleeveless mohair jersey with cowl neck

Sizes
To fit 32[34:36:38:40]in bust
Length to shoulder, 20½[21:21½:22:22½]in adjustable
The figures in brackets [] refer to the 34, 36, 38 and 40in sizes respectively
Tension
4 sts and 5 rows to 1in over rib worked on No.2 needles
Materials
7[8:9:9:10] balls Jaeger Mohair-Spun
One pair No.2 needles
One pair No.9 needles
One No.4·50 (ISR) crochet hook

Back
Using No.9 needles cast on 67[71:75:79:83] sts.
1st row K1, *P1, K1, rep from * to end.
2nd row P1, *K1, P1, rep from * to end.
Rep these 2 rows twice more.
Change to No.2 needles. Cont in rib until work measures 14in from beg, or required length to underarm ending with a WS row.
Shape armholes
Cast off 5 sts at beg of next 2 rows. Dec one st at each end of next and foll 2[2:3:3:4] alt rows. 51[55:57:61:63] sts. Cont without shaping until armholes measure 6[6½:7:7½:8]in from beg, ending with a WS row.
Shape neck
Next row Rib 17[18:19:20:21] sts, cast off 17[19: 19:21:21] sts, rib to end.
Complete this side first. Dec one st at neck edge on next and foll 2 alt rows. Cast off rem sts.
With WS of work facing, rejoin yarn to rem sts and

complete to match first side, reversing shaping.

Front
Work as given for back.

Collar
Using No.9 needles cast on 99[101:103:105:107] sts. Work 6 rows rib as given for back. Change to No.2 needles and cont in rib until work measures 6½in from beg. Cast off very loosely in rib.

To make up
Do not press. Join shoulder and side seams. Join collar seam, then sew round neck with seam to centre back. Using No.4·50 (ISR) hook work a row of dc round each armhole.

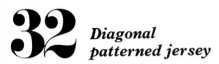

Diagonal patterned jersey

Sizes
To fit 32[34:36:38:40]in bust
Length to shoulder, 22[22½:23:23½:24]in
Sleeve seam, 6in
The figures in brackets [] refer to the 34, 36, 38 and 40in sizes respectively

Tension
7 sts and 9 rows to 1in over st st worked on No.10 needles

Materials
9[10:11:12:13] balls Robin Casino Crepe 4 ply
One pair No.10 needles
One pair No.12 needles
Set of 4 No.12 needles pointed at both ends

Back
Using No.12 needles cast on 110[118:126:134:142] sts.
1st row K2, *P2, K2, rep from * to end.
2nd row P2, *K2, P2, rep from * to end.
Rep these 2 rows until work measures 2in from beg, ending with a P row. Change to No.10 needles. Beg with a P row cont in st st until work measures 15½in from beg, ending with a P row.

Shape armholes
Cast off at beg of next and every row 6 sts twice and 2[3:3:4:4] sts twice. Dec one st at each end of next and foll 3[4:5:6:7] alt rows. 86[90:96:100:106] sts. Cont without shaping until armholes measure 6½[7:7½:8:8½]in from beg, ending with a P row.

Shape shoulders
Cast off at beg of next and every row 6[6:7:8:8] sts 6 times and 6[8:7:6:8] sts twice. Leave rem 38[38:40:40:42] sts on holder.

Front
Using No.12 needles cast on 110[118:126:134:142] sts. Work in rib as given for back for 2in, ending with a 1st row and inc 10[10:11:11:9] sts evenly across last row. 120[128:137:145:151] sts. Change to No.10 needles. Commence patt.
1st row (WS) P18[22:16:20:23] sts, *(P1, K1) 7 times, P1, K6, rep from * 3[3:4:4:4] times more, P to end.
2nd row K18[22:16:20:23] sts, *P5, yrn, P1, (K1, P1) 6 times, K first and 3rd sts on left hand needle tog and let first st drop off needle, P 2nd st then let 2nd and 3rd sts drop off needle – called Tw3 –, rep from * 3[3:4:4:4] times more, K to end.
3rd row P18[22:16:20:23] sts, K1, *rib 15, K6, rep from * 2[2:3:3:3] times more, rib 15, K5, P to end.
4th row K18[22:16:20:23] sts, P4, yrn, P1, *rib 12, Tw3, P5, yrn, P1, rep from * 2[2:3:3:3] times more, rib 12, Tw3, P1, K to end.
5th row P18[22:16:20:23] sts, K2, *rib 15, K6, rep from * 2[2:3:3:3] times more, rib 15, K4, P to end.

6th row K18[22:16:20:23] sts, P3, yrn, P1, *rib 12, Tw3, P5, yrn, P1, rep from * 2[2:3:3:3] times more, rib 12, Tw3, P2, K to end.
7th row P18[22:16:20:23] sts, K3, *rib 15, K6, rep from * 2[2:3:3:3] times more, rib 15, K3, P to end.
8th row K18[22:16:20:23] sts, P2, yrn, P1, *rib 12, Tw3, P5, yrn, P1, rep from * 2[2:3:3:3] times more, rib 12, Tw3, P3, K to end.
9th row P18[22:16:20:23] sts, K4, *rib 15, K6, rep from * 2[2:3:3:3] times more, rib 15, K2, P to end.
10th row K18[22:16:20:23] sts, P1, yrn, P1, *rib 12, Tw3, P5, yrn, P1, rep from * 2[2:3:3:3] times more, rib 12, Tw3, P4, K to end.
11th row P18[22:16:20:23] sts, K5, *rib 15, K6, rep from * 2[2:3:3:3] times more, rib 15, K1, P to end.
12th row K18[22:16:20:23] sts, yrn, P1, *rib 12, Tw3, P5, yrn, P1, rep from * 2[2:3:3:3] times more, rib 12, Tw3, P5, yon, K to end.
13th row P19[23:17:21:24] sts, *K6, rib 15, rep from * 3[3:4:4:4] times more, P to end.
14th row K18[22:16:20:23] sts, *rib 12, Tw3, P5, yrn, P1, rep from * 3[3:4:4:4] times more, K to end.
15th row P19[23:17:21:24] sts, K1, P1, *K6, rib 15, rep from * 2[2:3:3:3] times more, K6, rib 13, P to end.
16th row K18[22:16:20:23] sts, rib 10, Tw3, *P5, yrn, P1, rib 12, Tw3, rep from * 2[2:3:3:3] times more, P5, yrn, P1, K1, P1, K to end.
17th row P19[23:17:21:24] sts, (K1, P1) twice, *K6, rib 15, rep from * 2[2:3:3:3] times more, K6, rib 11, P to end.
18th row K18[22:16:20:23] sts, rib 8, Tw3, *P5, yrn, P1, rib 12, Tw3, rep from * 2[2:3:3:3] times more, P5, yrn, P1, rib 4, K to end.
19th row P19[23:17:21:24] sts, rib 6, *K6, rib 15, rep from * 2[2:3:3:3] times more, K6, rib 9, P to end.
20th row K18[22:16:20:23] sts, rib 6, Tw3, *P5, yrn, P1, rib 12, Tw3, rep from * 2[2:3:3:3] times more, P5, yrn, P1, rib 6, K to end.
21st row P19[23:17:21:24] sts, rib 8, *K6, rib 15, rep from * 2[2:3:3:3] times more, K6, rib 7, P to end.
22nd row K18[22:16:20:23] sts, rib 4, Tw3, *P5, yrn, P1, rib 12, Tw3, rep from * 2[2:3:3:3] times more, P5, yrn, P1, rib 8, K to end.
23rd row P19[23:17:21:24] sts, rib 10, *K6, rib 15, rep from * 2[2:3:3:3] times more, K6, rib 5, P to end.
24th row K18[22:16:20:23] sts, rib 2, Tw3, *P5, yrn, P1, rib 12, Tw3, rep from * 2[2:3:3:3] times more, P5, yrn, P1, rib 10, K to end.
25th row P19[23:17:21:24] sts, rib 12, *K6, rib 15, rep from * 2[2:3:3:3] times more, K6, rib 3, P to end.
26th row K18[22:16:20:23] sts, Tw3, *P5, yrn, P1, rib 12, Tw3, rep from * 2[2:3:3:3] times more, P5, yrn, P1, rib 12, K to end.
27th row P19[23:17:21:24] sts, rib 14, *K6, rib 15, rep from * 2[2:3:3:3] times more, K6, P1, P to end.
28th row K18[22:16:20:23] sts, P2 tog, P4, yrn, P1, *r.b 12, Tw3, P5, yrn, P1, rep from * 2[2:3:3:3] times more, rib 12, Tw3, K to end.
Rows 3 to 28 form patt. Cont in patt until work measures same as back to underarm, ending with a WS row.

Shape armholes
Keeping patt correct, cast off at each end of next and every row 6 sts twice and 2[3:3:4:4] sts twice. Dec one st at each end of next and foll 3[4:5:6:7] alt rows. 96[100:107:111:115] sts. Note that when working patt between 12th and 27th rows there will be one more st. Cont without shaping until armholes measure 4½[5:5½:6:6½]in from beg, ending with a WS row.

Shape neck
Next row Patt 37[39:41:43:45] sts, turn and leave rem sts on holder.
Cast off 2 sts at beg of next and foll 2 alt rows, then

dec one st at neck edge on next 4 alt rows. Cont without shaping until armhole measures same as back to shoulder, ending at armhole edge.

Shape shoulder
Cast off 6[7:7:8:9] sts at beg of next and foll 2 alt rows. Work 1 row. Cast off rem 9[8:10:9:8] sts.
With RS of work facing, sl first 22[22:25:25:27] sts on holder, rejoin yarn to rem sts and patt to end, noting that when working patt between 12th and 27th rows there will be one more st. Complete to match first side, reversing shaping.

Sleeves
Using No.12 needles cast on 66[66:70:70:74] sts. Work 2½in rib as given for back, ending with a 2nd row and inc one st at each end of last row on 34 and 38in sizes only. 66[68:70:72:74] sts. Change to No.10 needles. Beg with a K row cont in st st, inc one st at each end of 5th and every foll 6th row until there are 72[74:76:78:80] sts. Cont without shaping until sleeve measures 6in from beg, ending with a P row.

Shape top
Cast off 6 sts at beg of next 2 rows. Dec one st at each end of next and every alt row until 34 sts rem. Cast off at beg of next and every row 2 sts 6 times, 3 sts twice and 4 sts twice. Cast off rem 8 sts.

Neckband
Join shoulder seams. Using set of 4 No.12 needles and with RS of work facing, K across sts on back neck holder, K up 22 sts down side of neck, K across sts on front neck holder dec one st in centre on 36, 38 and 40in sizes only, then K up 22 sts up other side of neck. 104[104:108:108:112] sts. Note that if sts were left on holder for front neck between 12th and 27th patt rows, dec one more st. Work 1in in rounds of K2, P2 rib. Cast off in rib.

To make up
Press each piece under a damp cloth with a warm iron. Join side and sleeve seams. Set in sleeves. Press seams.

Ribbed polo neck jersey

Sizes
To fit 32[34:36:38]in bust
Length to shoulder, 24[25:26:27]in
Sleeve seam, 17[17½:18:18½]in
The figures in brackets [ ] refer to the 34, 36 and 38in sizes respectively

Tension
6 sts and 7½ rows to 1in over rib patt worked on No. 8 needles

Materials
Lee Target Motoravia Double Knitting 24[25:26:27] balls
One pair No. 8 needles
One pair No. 10 needles

Back
Using No. 10 needles cast on 102[106:114:118] sts.
1st row K2, *P2, K2, rep from * to end.
2nd row P2, *K2, P2, rep from * to end.
Rep these 2 rows until work measures 4in from beg, ending with a 2nd row and inc one st in centre of last row on 34 and 38in sizes, and dec one st in centre of last row on 32 and 36in sizes. 101 [107:113:119] sts. Change to No. 8 needles.
Next row K2, *P1, K2, rep from * to end.
Next row P2, *K1, P2, rep from * to end.
Rep last 2 rows until work measures 16½[17:17½:18]in from beg, ending with a WS row.

Shape armholes
Cast off 3 sts at beg of next 8 rows. 77[83:89:95] sts. Cont without shaping until armholes measure

$7\frac{1}{2}[8:8\frac{1}{2}:9]$in from beg, ending with a WS row.

Shape shoulders

Cast off at beg of next and every row 5[6:6:7] sts 6 times and 6[5:7:6] sts twice. Cast off rem 35[37:39:41] sts.

Front

Work as given for back until 12 rows less than back to armholes, ending with a WS row.

Divide for neck

Next row Patt 50[53:56:59] sts, turn and leave rem sts on holder.

Next row Patt to end.

Next row Patt to last 4 sts, P2 tog, K2.

Next row P2, K1, patt to end.

Next row Patt to last 3 sts, P1, K2.

Next row P2, K1, patt to end.

Rep last 4 rows once more, then first 2 of these last 4 rows once.

Shape armhole

Cast off 3 sts at beg of next and foll 3 alt rows, *at the same time* cont to dec at neck edge on every 4th row until 21[23:25:27] sts rem. Cont without shaping until work measures same as back to shoulder, ending at armhole edge.

Shape shoulder

Cast off 5[6:6:7] sts at beg of next and foll 2 alt rows. Work 1 row. Cast off rem 6[5:7:6] sts. With RS of work facing, rejoin yarn to rem sts, K2 tog, patt to end.

Next row Patt to end.

Next row K2, P2 tog, patt to end.

Next row Patt to last 3 sts, K1, P2.

Complete to match first side, reversing all shaping.

Sleeves

Using No. 10 needles cast on 50[54:54:58] sts. Work first 2 rows rib as given for back until work measures 4in from beg, ending with a 2nd row and dec one st in centre of last row on 34in size, inc one st at each end of last row on 36in size and inc one st in centre of last row on 38in size. 50[53:56:59] sts.

Change to No. 8 needles and cont in patt as given for back, inc one st at each end of 7th and every foll 8th row and working extra sts into patt, until there are 74[77:80:83] sts. Cont without shaping until sleeve measures $17[17\frac{1}{2}:18:18\frac{1}{2}]$in from beg, ending with a WS row.

Shape top

Cast off 2 sts at beg of every row until 10[9:8:7] sts rem. Cast off.

Front insert and collar

Using No. 8 needles cast on 6 sts.

1st row K2, P2, K2.

2nd row P2, K2, P2.

Cont in rib, inc one st at each end of next and every foll 4th row and working the extra sts into rib patt, until there are 38[40:42:44] sts. Cont without shaping until work measures $6\frac{1}{2}[7:7\frac{1}{2}:8]$in from beg, ending with a WS row. Leave sts for time being. Break off yarn.

Using No. 10 needles cast on 48[50:52:54] sts. Leave sts for time being. Break off yarn.

Using No. 10 needles cast on 12 sts.

Next row Rib 12 sts, rib across 38[40:42:44] sts on needle, then rib across 48[50:52:54] sts on needle. 98[102:106:110] sts.

Cont in K2, P2 rib until collar measures 4in from cast on sts. Change to No. 8 needles and cont in rib for a further 8in.

Cast off loosely in rib.

To make up

Press each piece lightly under a damp cloth with a warm iron. Join shoulder seams. Set in sleeves. Join side and sleeve seams. Join seam of collar. Sew insert and collar to neck edge, having collar seam to left shoulder seam and point of insert to centre front neck.

Press seams.

34 *Aran tunic with slit sides*

Sizes

To fit 34[36:38:40:42]in bust

Length to shoulder, $27[27\frac{1}{4}:27\frac{1}{2}:27\frac{3}{4}:28]$in

The figures in brackets [] refer to the 36, 38, 40 and 42in sizes respectively

Tension

4 sts and 6 rows to 1in over st st worked on No.6 needles

Materials

9[10:11:11:12] balls Mahony Blarney Bainin Quicker Knitting

One pair No.6 needles

One pair No.8 needles

Cable needle

12 small wooden beads for belt

Front panel

Using No.6 needles cast on 55[57:59:61:63] sts. Work 4 rows K1, P1 rib. Commence patt.

1st row (RS) (K1, P1) twice, P2[3:4:5:6] sts, sl next 2 sts on to cable needle and hold at back of work, K2 sts from left hand needle then K 2 from cable needle – called C4B –, P1, K into front then into back of next st – called M2 –, P1, M2, (P1, K1, P1, K1) all into next st, turn and K4, turn and P4, lift 2nd, 3rd and 4th sts over 1st st and off needle – called B1 –, P1, M2, P1, M2, P6, sl next 3 sts on to cable needle and hold at front of work, K2 sts from left hand needle, sl 1st st on cable needle on to left hand needle and P it, then K2 sts from cable needle – called Cr5 –, P6, M2, P1, M2, P1, B1, M2, P1, M2, P1, sl next 2 sts on to cable needle and hold at front of work, K2 sts from left hand needle then K2 sts from cable needle – called C4F –, P2[3:4:5:6] sts, (P1, K1) twice.

2nd row (P1, K1) twice, K2[3:4:5:6] sts, P4, K1, P2 tog, K1, P2 tog, K2, P2 tog, K1, P2 tog, K6, P2, K1, P2, K6, P2 tog, K1, P2 tog, K2, P2 tog, K1, P2 tog, K1, P4, K2[3:4:5:6] sts, (K1, P1) twice.

3rd row (K1, P1) twice, P2[3:4:5:6] sts, K4, P1, M2, P1, M2, P2, M2, P1, M2, P5, sl next st on to cable needle and hold at back of work, K2 sts from left hand needle then P1 from cable needle – called C3B –, P1, sl next 2 sts on to cable needle and hold at front of work, P1 from left hand needle then K2 sts from cable needle – called C3F –, P5, M2, P1, M2, P2, M2, P1, M2, P1, K4, P2[3:4:5:6] sts, (P1, K1) twice.

4th row (P1, K1) twice, K2[3:4:5:6] sts, P4, K1, P2 tog, K1, P2 tog, K2, P2 tog, K1, P2 tog, K5, P2, K3, P2, K5, P2 tog, K1, P2 tog, K2, P2 tog, K1, P2 tog, K1, P4, K2[3:4:5:6] sts, (K1, P1) twice.

5th row (K1, P1) twice, P2[3:4:5:6] sts, K4, P1, M2, P1, M2, P2, M2, P1, M2, P4, C3B, P3, C3F, P4, M2, P1, M2, P2, M2, P1, M2, P1, K4, P2[3:4:5:6] sts, (P1, K1) twice.

6th row (P1, K1) twice, K2[3:4:5:6] sts, P4, K1, P2 tog, K1, P2 tog, K2, P2 tog, K1, P2 tog, K4, P2, K5, P2, K4, P2 tog, K1, P2 tog, K2, P2 tog, K1, P2 tog, K1, P4, K2[3:4:5:6] sts, (K1, P1) twice.

7th row (K1, P1) twice, P2[3:4:5:6] sts, C4B, P1, M2, P1, M2, P1, B1, M2, P1, M2, P3, C3B, P2, K into front, then into back, then into front, then into back of next st – called M4 –, P2, C3F, P3, M2, P1, M2, B1, P1, M2, P1, M2, P1, C4F, P2[3:4:5:6] sts, (P1, K1) twice.

8th row (P1, K1) twice, K2[3:4:5:6] sts, P4, K1, P2 tog, K1, P2 tog, K2, P2 tog, K1, P2 tog, K3, P2, K3, P4, K3, P2, K3, P2 tog, K1, P2 tog, K2, P2 tog, K1, P2 tog, K1, P4, K2[3:4:5:6] sts, (K1, P1) twice.

9th row (K1, P1) twice, P2[3:4:5:6] sts, K4, P1, M2, P1, M2, P2, M2, P1, M2, P2, C3B, P3, K4, P3, C3F, P2, M2, P1, M2, P2, M2, P1, M2, P1, K4, P2[3:4:5:6] sts, (P1, K1) twice.

10th row (P1, K1) twice, K2[3:4:5:6] sts, P4, K1, P2 tog, K2, P2 tog, K1, P2 tog, K2, P2, K4, P4 tog, K4, P2, K2, P2 tog, K1, P2 tog, K1, P4, K2[3:4:5:6] sts, (K1, P1) twice.

11th row (K1, P1) twice, P2[3:4:5:6] sts, K4, P1, M2, P1, M2, P2, M2, P1, M2, P1, C3B, P1, M4, P5, M4, P1, C3F, P1, M2, P1, M2, P2, M2, P1, M2, P1, K4, P2[3:4:5:6] sts, (P1, K1) twice.

12th row (P1, K1) twice, K2[3:4:5:6] sts, P4, K1, P2 tog, K1, P2 tog, K2, P2 tog, K1, P2 tog, K1, P2, K2, P4, K5, P4, K2, P2, K1, P2 tog, K1, P2 tog, K2, P2 tog, K1, P2 tog, K1, P4, K2[3:4:5:6] sts, (K1, P1) twice.

13th row (K1, P1) twice, P2[3:4:5:6] sts, C4B, P1, M2, P1, M2, B1, P1, M2, P1, M2, P1, C3F, P1, K4, P5, K4, P1, C3B, P1, M2, P1, M2, P1, B1, M2, P1, M2, P1, C4F, P2[3:4:5:6] sts, (P1, K1) twice.

14th row (P1, K1) twice, K2[3:4:5:6] sts, P4, K1, P2 tog, K1, P2 tog, K2, P2 tog, K1, P2 tog, K2, P2, K1, P4 tog, K5, P4 tog, K1, P2, K2, P2 tog, K1, P2 tog, K1, P2 tog, K1, P4, K2[3:4:5:6] sts, (K1, P1) twice.

15th row (K1, P1) twice, P2[3:4:5:6] sts, K4, P1, M2, P1, M2, P2, M2, P1, M2, P2, C3F, P3, M4, P3, C3B, P2, M2, P1, M2, P2, M2, P1, M2, P1, K4, P2[3:4:5:6] sts, (P1, K1) twice.

16th row As 8th.

17th row (K1, P1) twice, P2[3:4:5:6] sts, K4, P1, M2, P1, M2, P2, M2, P1, M2, P3, C3F, P2, K4, P2, C3B, P3, M2, P1, M2, P2, M2, P1, M2, P1, K4, P2[3:4:5:6] sts, (P1, K1) twice.

18th row (P1, K1) twice, K2[3:4:5:6] sts, P4, K1, P2 tog, K1, P2 tog, K2, P2 tog, K1, P2 tog, K4, P2, K2, P4 tog, K2, P2, K4, P2 tog, K1, P2 tog, K2, P2 tog, K1, P2 tog, K1, P4, K2[3:4:5:6] sts, (K1, P1) twice.

19th row (K1, P1) twice, P2[3:4:5:6] sts, C4B, P1, M2, P1, M2, P1, B1, M2, P1, M2, P4, C3F, P3, C3B, P4, M2, P1, M2, B1, P1, M2, P1, M2, P1, C4F, P2[3:4:5:6] sts, (P1, K1) twice.

20th row As 4th.

21st row (K1, P1) twice, P2[3:4:5:6] sts, K4, P1, M2, P1, M2, P2, M2, P1, M2, P5, C3F, P1, C3B, P5, M2, P1, M2, P2, M2, P1, M2, P1, K4, P2[3:4:5:6] sts, (P1, K1) twice.

22nd row As 2nd.

23rd row (K1, P1) twice, P2[3:4:5:6] sts, K4, P1, M2, P1, M2, P2, M2, P1, M2, P6, K2, P1, K2, P6, M2, P1, M2, P2, M2, P1, M2, P1, K4, P2[3:4:5:6] sts, (P1, K1) twice.

24th row (P1, K1) twice, K2[3:4:5:6] sts, P4, K1, P2 tog, K1, P2 tog, K2, P2 tog, K1, P2 tog, K6, P5, K6, P2 tog, K1, P2 tog, K2, P2 tog, K1, P2 tog, K1, P4, K2[3:4:5:6] sts, (K1, P1) twice.

These 24 rows form patt. Cont in patt until work measures 6in from beg, ending with a WS row.

Next row Inc in first st, P5[6:7:8:9] sts, patt to last 6[7:8:9:10] sts, P5[6:7:8:9] sts, inc in last st. 57[59:61:63:65] sts.

Keeping 7[8:9:10:11] sts at each end in reversed st st, cont in patt until work measures $24\frac{3}{4}[25:25\frac{1}{4}:25\frac{1}{2}:25\frac{3}{4}]$in from beg, ending with a WS row.**

Shape neck

Next row Patt 20[21:22:23:24] sts, turn and leave rem sts on holder.

Dec one st at neck edge on next 3 rows, then dec one st at same edge on every alt row until 14[15:16:17:18] sts rem. Cont without shaping until work measures $27[27\frac{1}{4}:27\frac{1}{2}:27\frac{3}{4}:28]$in from beg, ending at armhole edge.

Shape shoulder

Cast off 7 sts at beg of next row. Work 1 row. Cast off rem 7[8:9:10:11] sts.

With RS of work facing, sl next 17 sts on to holder, rejoin yarn to rem sts and patt to end. Complete to match first side, reversing shaping.

Back panel

Work as given for front panel to **. Cont in patt until work measures same as front to shoulder, ending with a WS row.

Shape shoulders
Cast off at beg of next and every row 7 sts twice and 7[8:9:10:11] sts twice. Leave rem 29 sts on holder.

Side panel (make 2)
Using No.6 needles cast on 29[31:33:35:37] sts. Work 4 rows K1, P1 rib, dec one st in centre of last row. 28[30:32:34:36] sts. Commence patt.
1st row (RS) (K1, P1) twice, P6[7:8:9:10] sts, M2, P1, M2, B1, P1, M2, P1, M2, P6[7:8:9:10] sts, (P1, K1) twice.
2nd row (P1, K1) twice, K6[7:8:9:10] sts, P2 tog, K1, P2 tog, K2, P2 tog, K1, P2 tog, K6[7:8:9:10] sts, (K1, P1) twice.
3rd row (K1, P1) twice, P6[7:8:9:10] sts, M2, P1, M2, P2, M2, P1, M2, P6[7:8:9:10] sts, (P1, K1) twice.
Rep 2nd and 3rd rows once more, then 2nd row once.
7th row (K1, P1) twice, P6[7:8:9:10] sts, M2, P1, M2, P1, B1, M2, P1, M2, P6[7:8:9:10] sts, (P1, K1) twice.
Rep 2nd and 3rd rows twice more, then 2nd row once.
These 12 rows form patt. Cont in patt until work measures 6in from beg, ending with a WS row.
Next row Inc in first st, P9[10:11:12:13] sts, patt 8, P9[10:11:12:13] sts, inc in last st. 30[32:34:36: 38] sts.
Keeping 11[12:13:14:15] sts in reversed st st at each end, cont in patt until work measures 8in from beg, ending with a RS row.

Shape sides
Next row K9[10:11:12:13] sts, sl 1, K1, psso, patt 8, K2 tog, K to end.
Work 1 row.
Next row K8[9:10:11:12] sts, sl 1, K1, psso, patt 8, K2 tog, K to end.
Work 1 row.
Cont dec in this way on next and every alt row until 12[14:16:18:20] sts rem. Cont without shaping until work measures 12½in from beg, ending with a RS row.
Next row K2[3:4:5:6] sts, pick up loop lying between sts and K tbl – called inc 1 –, patt 8, inc 1, K to end.
Work 3 rows.
Next row K3[4:5:6:7] sts, inc 1, patt 8, inc 1, K to end.
Work 3 rows.
Cont inc in this way on next and every 4th row until there are 26[28:30:32:34] sts. Cont without shaping until work measures 19in from beg, ending with a WS row.

Shape underarm
Next row Patt 9[10:10:11:11] sts, turn and leave rem sts on holder.
Dec one st at beg of next and at same edge on every row until all sts are worked off.
With RS of work facing, sl first 8[8:10:10:12] sts on holder, rejoin yarn to rem sts and patt to end.
Dec one st at end of next and at same edge on every row until all sts are worked off.

Armbands
Press pieces under a damp cloth with a warm iron. Join side panels to back and front panels from top of ribbing to slits. Using No.8 needles and with RS of work facing, beg at shoulder and K up 43[45:47: 49:51] sts down armhole, K across sts on holder, dec one st in centre, and K up 43[45:47:49:51] sts to shoulder. 93[97:103:107:113] sts. Work 4 rows K1, P1 rib, working 3 sts tog in centre of every alt row. Cast off in rib, still dec at centre.

Neckband
Join right shoulder and armband seam. Using No.8 needles and with RS of work facing K across 29 sts at centre back neck inc in first st, K up 18[20:22: 24:26] sts down front neck, K17 sts on holder and K up 19[21:23:25:27] sts up front neck. 84[88:92:

96:100] sts. Work 4 rows K1, P1 rib. Cast off in rib.

To make up
Join left shoulder and armband seam. Press seams.

Make belt
Cut 12 lengths of yarn 90in long. (Take 2 ends tog and knot at one end, thread on bead) 6 times. Tie tog 10in from beaded end. Form into 3 strands and plait to within 16in of other end. Knot tog at end of plait, (take 2 ends tog, thread on bead and knot at end) 6 times. Trim ends.

Beret and scarf

Sizes
Beret to fit an average head
Scarf 8in wide by 68in long
Tension
6 sts and 12 rows to 1in over g st worked on No. 9 needles
Materials
Jaeger Celtic-Spun
Beret 1 ball each of 4 colours, A, B, C and D
Scarf 2 balls each of 4 colours, A, B, C and D
One pair No. 9 needles

Beret
Using No. 9 needles and A, cast on 44 sts.
1st row (RS) K to end.
2nd row K40 sts, turn.
3rd row K32 sts, turn.
4th row K28 sts, turn.
5th row K24 sts, turn.
6th row K20 sts, turn.
7th row As 5th.
8th row As 4th.
9th row K36 sts to end.
10th row As 2nd.
11th row K44 sts to end.
12th row K44 sts to end. Do not break yarn.
Rep these 12 rows using B, C and D. These 48 rows form patt and are rep throughout. Work patt rows 6 times more Cast off.

To make up
Darn in all ends. With WS of work facing, join back seam and using running sts, draw up centre crown. Press seam lightly. Using A, B, C and D make a pompon and sew to top.

Scarf
Using No. 9 needles and A, cast on 360 sts. Work in stripes of 12 rows g st using A, B, C and D. Rep these 48 rows once more.
Cast off loosely.

To make up
Darn in all ends. With WS of work facing and using running sts, draw up each short end of scarf and fasten off. Make 2 pompons as given for beret and sew one to each short end.

Sleeveless or puff sleeved hug-me-tight and hat

Sizes
To fit a 32[34:36:38:40]in bust
Length at centre back, 19½[19¾:20:20¼:20½]in adjustable
Sleeve seam, 5in adjustable
The figures in brackets [ ] refer to the 34, 36, 38 and 40in sizes respectively

Tension
7½ sts and 8 rows to 1in over patt when pressed worked on No. 8 needles and using 2 ends of yarn
Materials
Twilley's Mohair
Sleeveless version 8[9:9:10:10] balls
Puff sleeved version 12[13:13:14:14] balls
Hat 2 balls
One pair No. 8 needles
One pair No. 10 needles
Six buttons
Note
Yarn is used double throughout. Where an odd number is given in the materials section, wind last ball into 2 separate balls.

Back
Using No. 10 needles and 2 ends of yarn, cast on 117[125:133:141:149] sts.
1st row Sl 1, *P1, K1, rep from * to end.
2nd row Sl 1, *K1, P1, rep from * to last 2 sts, K2.
Rep these 2 rows until work measures 4in from beg, ending with a 2nd row.
Next row Inc in first st, rib to last 2 sts, inc in next st, K1. 119[127:135:143:151] sts.
Change to No. 8 needles. Commence patt. **.
1st row (WS) Sl 1, K1 tbl, *insert needle p-wise into next 3 sts as if to P3 tog but P1, K1 tbl, P1 all into these 3 sts and sl them off left hand needle – called M3 –, K1 tbl, rep from * to last st, K1.
2nd row Sl 1, P to last st, K1.
These 2 rows form patt. Cont in patt until work measures 11in from beg for sleeveless version, or 12in for puff sleeved version, or required length to underarm ending with a WS row.

Shape armholes
Keeping patt correct cast off 7[7:8:8:9] sts loosely at beg of next 2 rows. Dec one st at each end of next 6 rows, then each end of next and every alt row until 83[87:91:95:99] sts rem for sleeveless version, or 91[95:99:103:107] sts for puff sleeved version. Cont without shaping until armholes measure 7¾[8:8¼:8½:8¾]in from beg for sleeveless version, or 6¾[7:7¼:7½:7¾]in for puff sleeved version, ending with a WS row.

Shape shoulders
Cast off loosely at beg of next and every row 6 sts 4 times for sleeveless version, or 8 sts 4 times for puff sleeved version, and 7[8:9:10:11] sts twice for both versions.
Leave rem sts on holder.

Front
Work as given for back to **.
Divide for front
1st row (WS) Sl 1, K1 tbl, *M3, K1 tbl, rep from * 12[13:14:15:16] times more, K1, turn.
Complete right front on these 55[59:63:67:71] sts.
2nd row Sl 1, P to last st, K1.
Cont in patt until work measures same as back to underarm, ending at armhole edge.

Shape armhole
Keeping patt correct cast off 7[7:8:8:9] sts loosely at beg of next row. Work 1 row. Dec one st at armhole edge on next 6 rows, then next and every alt row until 37[39:41:43:45] sts rem for sleeveless version, or 41[43:45:47:49] sts for puff sleeved version. Cont without shaping until armhole measures 3[3¼:3½:3¾:4]in from beg for sleeveless version, or 2[2¼:2½:2¾:3]in for puff sleeved version, ending at front edge.

Shape neck
Next row Sl 1, patt 7[8:9:10:11] sts and sl these 8[9:10:11:12] sts on to holder and leave for centre neck, patt to last st, K1.
Cont in patt, dec one st at neck edge on every row 10 times in all. 19[20:21:22:23] sts for sleeveless version, or 23[24:25:26:27] sts for puff sleeved version. Cont without shaping until armhole measures same as back to shoulder, ending at armhole edge.

Shape shoulder

Cast off 6 sts loosely at beg of next and foll alt row for sleeveless version, or 8 sts loosely at beg of next and foll alt row for puff sleeved version. Work 1 row. Cast off rem 7[8:9:10:11] sts.
With WS of work facing, sl next 9 sts on to holder and leave for front band. Rejoin yarn to rem sts and complete to match right front, reversing all shapings.

Puff sleeves

Using No. 10 needles and 2 ends of yarn cast on 75[79:83:87:91] sts. Work 1in rib as given for back, ending with a 2nd row.
Next row Rib 2[4:6:8:10] sts, *inc in next st, rib 1, rep from * to last 3[5:7:9:11] sts, inc in next st, rib to end. 111[115:119:123:127] sts. Change to No. 8 needles. Work in patt as given for back until sleeve measures 5in from beg, or required length to underarm ending with a WS row.

Shape top

Keeping patt correct cast off 7[7:8:8:9] sts loosely at beg of next 2 rows. Dec one st at each end of next 6 rows, then each end of next and every alt row until 61 sts rem, then each end of every row until 45 sts rem, ending with a RS row.

32, 36 and 40in sizes only

Next row Sl 1, *K3 tog, K1 tbl, rep from * to end. 23 sts.

34 and 38in sizes only

Next row Sl 1, P1, *K1 tbl, K3 tog, rep from * to last 3 sts, K1 tbl, P1, K1. 25 sts.

All sizes

Next row Sl 1, *P2 tog, rep from * to end. Cast off loosely.

Buttonhole band

Mark positions for 6 buttons on left front, first to come 1in above waist ribbing and 6th to come in neckband. Using No. 10 needles and with WS of work facing, rejoin 2 ends of yarn to sts on holder and work in rib as given for back, making buttonholes as markers are reached as foll:
Next row (RS row) Rib 3, cast off 2 sts, rib 4.
Next row Rib to end, casting on 2 sts above those cast off in previous row.
Work in rib until band measures same as right front opening to neck shaping, when very slightly stretched. Leave sts on holder.

Button band

Using No. 10 needles and 2 ends of yarn, cast on 9 sts. Work as given for buttonhole band omitting buttonholes.

Neckband

Join shoulder seams. Using No. 10 needles and 2 ends of yarn and with RS of work facing, rib across sts of buttonhole band and centre neck holders, K up 38[40:42:44:46] sts, rib across sts of back neck holder, K up 38[40:42:44:46] sts, rib across sts of centre neck holder and button band holder. 155[163:171:179:187] sts.
Work 1in rib as given for back, making button hole as before on 4th and 5th rows.
Cast off in rib.

Armbands for sleeveless version

Using No. 10 needles and 2 ends of yarn and with RS of work facing, K up 139[143:147:151:155] sts round armhole. Work 1in rib as given for back, dec one st at each end of every alt row.
Cast off in rib.

To make up

Press each piece lightly on WS under a damp cloth with a warm iron, omitting ribbing. Join side seams. Join sleeve seams for puff sleeved version and set in sleeves. Oversew front bands to fronts, catching down button band at bottom of button-hole band.
Press seams. Sew on buttons.

Hat

Using No. 10 needles and 2 ends of yarn, cast on 135 sts. Work 1in rib as given for back, ending with a 2nd row.
Next row Rib 1, *rib 10, inc in next st, rep from * to last 2 sts, rib 2. 147 sts.
Change to No. 8 needles. Cont in patt as given for back until work measures 5½in from beg, ending with a RS row.

Shape top

Next row Sl 1, K1 tbl, *insert needle p-wise into next 3 sts as if to P3 tog but P1, K1 tbl into them and sl off left hand needle, K1 tbl, rep from * to last st, K1. 111 sts.
Next row Sl 1, P to last st, K1.
Next row Sl 1, K1 tbl, *insert needle p-wise into next 2 sts as if to P2 tog but P1, K1 tbl into them and sl off left hand needle, K1 tbl, rep from * to last st, K1.
Rep last 2 rows twice more, then first of these rows once more.
Next row Sl 1, K1 tbl, *P2 tog, K1 tbl, rep from * to last st, K1. 75 sts.
Next row Sl 1, *P2 tog, rep from * to end. 38 sts.
Next row Sl 1, *P2 tog, rep from * to last st, K1. 20 sts.
Next row *P2 tog, rep from * to end. 10 sts.
Break yarn and thread through rem sts, draw up and fasten off.

To make up

Press as given for top. Join back seam. Press seam.

37 *Toreador bolero*

Sizes

To fit 34/36in bust
Length to shoulder, 22in

Tension

Small flower motif measures 2in across worked on No.4·50 (ISR) crochet hook

Materials

5 balls Twilley's Stalite in main shade, A
1 ball each in contrast colours B, C and D
One No.4·50 (ISR) crochet hook

Small flower

Using No.4·50 (ISR) hook and A, make 8ch. Join with a ss into first ch to form circle.
1st round 2ch, work 13dc into circle. Join with a ss into 2nd of first 2ch.
2nd round 1ch, *work 3tr into next st, 1dc into next st, rep from * to end, ending with 3tr in last st. Join with a ss to first 1ch. Fasten off. Make approx 149 more small flowers in A, 8 in B, 8 in C and 2 in D.

Small rose

Using No.4·50 (ISR) hook and D, make 6ch. Join with a ss into first ch to form circle.

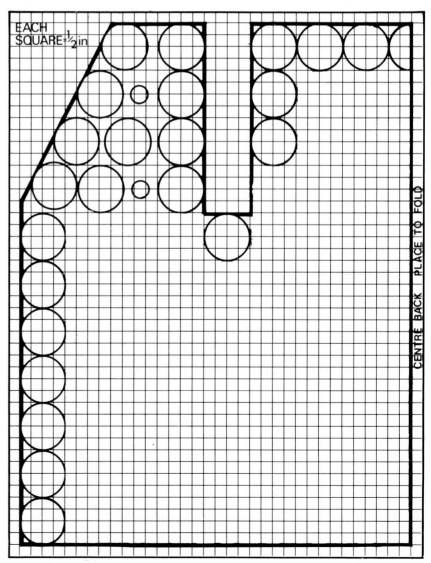

▲**37.** *Graph shows one front, armhole space and half of back. Scale: 1 square = ½ inch*

1st round 2ch, work 9dc into circle. Join with a ss to 2nd of first 2ch.
2nd round As 2nd round of small flower.
3rd round *3ch, insert hook from back of work round stem of dc and work 1dc – called 1dcB –, rep from * 4 times more, working last 1dcB into ss at end of previous round.
4th round Into each 3ch loop work 5tr and 1dc.
5th round *4ch, 1dcB, rep from * 4 times more, working last 1dcB into last 1dcB of 3rd round.
6th round Into each 4ch loop work 4tr, 2ch, 3tr and 1dc. Fasten off.
Make another small rose in same way.

Large rose
Using No.4·50 (ISR) hook and D, make 8ch. Join with a ss into first ch to form circle. Work first 2 rounds as given for small flower.
3rd round (3ch, 1dcB) 7 times, working last 1dcB into ss at end of previous round.
4th round As 4th round of small rose.
5th round (4ch, 1dcB) 7 times, working last 1dcB into last 1dcB of 3rd round.
6th round Into each 4ch loop work 7tr and 1dc.
7th round (6ch, 1dcB) 7 times, working last 1dcB into last 1dcB of 5th round.
8th round Into each 6ch loop work 6tr, 2ch, 5tr and 1dc. Fasten off.
Make another large rose in same way.

Small rings
Using No.4·50 (ISR) hook and A, make 6ch. Join with a ss to first ch to form circle.
1st round As 1st round of small flower. Fasten off.
Make approx 11 more in same way.

To make up
Pin out flowers and press under a damp cloth with a warm iron. Make a paper patt from diagram. Lay flowers on to patt, as foll: make an outline with flowers in A having 11 up each front edge, 2 at shoulder and 4 down each side of armhole, 1 at bottom edge of armhole and 7 across top of back. Fill in whole of back with flowers in A, having 7 lines of 11 flowers. Place 1 large and 1 small rose on each front and fill rem of fronts with flowers in A, B, C and D, using small rings to fill out spaces, as required. Join flowers with a short stem by making 2 sts into each flower, leaving a bare ¼in between them, then working 2 buttonhole sts over the stem. Join shoulder seams. If required, work round armhole edges, working dc into each flower and ch between them. Press.

38 *Crochet triangular shawl*

Size
Approx 63in by 33in plus fringe
Tension
Each square motif measures 3in by 3in worked on No.3·50 (ISR) crochet hook
Materials
5 balls Jaeger Celtic-Spun in main shade, A
5 balls Jaeger Celtic-Spun in contrast, B
4 balls Jaeger Celtic-Spun in contrast, C
One No.3·50 (ISR) crochet hook

Square motif
Using No.3·50 (ISR) hook and A, make 6ch. Join with a ss to first ch to form circle.
1st round 2ch, work 9dc into circle. Join with a ss to 2nd of first 2ch. 10 sts.
2nd round 3ch, work 1tr in same place, 2 tr into each st to end. Join with a ss to 3rd of first 3ch. 20 sts.
3rd round 7ch, *miss 4 sts, work 6tr into next st, 4ch, rep from * twice more, miss 4 sts, work

5tr into last st. Join with a ss to 3rd of first 7ch.
4th round 1ch, *work 4dc into 4ch loop, work 8tr between 3rd and 4th tr of 6tr gr, rep from * 3 times more. Join with a ss to first ch.
5th round 1ch, *1dc into each of next 4dc, 5ch, work 1dc into 4th tr, 1ch, work 1dc into next tr, 5ch, rep from * 3 times more. Join with a ss to first ch. Fasten off. Darn in ends.
Work 120 more square motifs in same way, making 41 more in A, 44 in B and 35 in C, or varying colours as required.

To make up
Join square motifs tog in required colour sequence, making one strip of 21 squares, one of 19 squares, one of 17 squares, and so on, ending with one square.
Work border
Using No.3·50 (ISR) hook, A and with RS of work facing, rejoin yarn to 1ch at front corner and work along two short sides, as foll:
1st row *12ch, work 1dc into 2nd of 4dc at side of square, 1ch, work 1dc into 1ch at corner, 12ch, work 1dc into 1ch at corner, 12ch, work 1dc into 2nd of next 4dc, 1ch, work 1dc into next dc, work 1 dc into 1ch at corner, 1ch, work 1dc into 1ch at corner of next square, rep from * round the 2 sides of each square along one edge, work in same way round 3 sides of square at centre, then work in same way along other edge. Fasten off. Turn.
2nd row (WS) Rejoin yarn into first 12ch loop, work 1dc into this loop, (12ch, work 1dc into next 12ch loop) 3 times, 2ch, work 1dc into first 12ch loop of next square, cont in this way along both edges working 5 loops round square at centre. Fasten off. Turn.
3rd row (RS) Rejoin yarn into first 12ch loop, work 1dc into this loop, *(12ch, work 1dc into next 12ch loop) twice, 12ch to stretch across angle between 2 squares, work 1dc into next 12ch loop, rep from * along both edges working 4 loops round square at centre. Fasten off. Turn.
4th row Rejoin yarn into first 12ch loop, work 1dc into this loop, *12ch, work 1dc into next 12ch loop, rep from * along both edges working 3 loops round square at centre. Fasten off. Turn.
5th row As 4th row working 3 loops round square at centre by working twice into the centre loop. Fasten off.
Pin out and press under a damp cloth with a warm iron.
Fringe Cut B and C into 16in lengths. Taking 3 strands of each colour tog at a time, knot into each loop along border, using alt colours. Trim fringe.

39 *Cardigan with Fair Isle yoke*

Sizes
To fit 34[36:38:40]in bust
Length to shoulder, 21½[22:22½:23]in
Sleeve seam, 16½[17½:18½:19½]in
The figures in brackets [] refer to the 36, 38 and 40in sizes respectively
Tension
6½ sts and 8½ rows to 1in over st st worked on No.10 needles
Materials
H & O Shetland Fleece distributed by Templetons
10[11:12:13] balls main shade, A
1 ball each contrast colours B, C, D, E and F
1 ball of additional contrast colour, if required, instead of A as background colour of yoke
One pair No.10 needles, one pair No.12 needles
Five stitch holders
Ten buttons

Back
Using No.12 needles and A, cast on 109[113:117:121] sts. Work in K1, P1 rib for 4in. Change to No.10 needles. Beg with a K row cont in st st, inc one st at each end of 7th and every foll 8th row until there are 115[121:127:133] sts. Cont without shaping until work measures 15in from beg, ending with a P row.
Shape armholes
Cast off 6 sts at beg of next 2 rows. 103[109:115:121] sts.
36, 38 and 40in sizes only
Dec one st at each end of next and every alt row until 103 sts rem, ending with a P row.
All sizes
Next row K2 tog, K33 sts, K2 tog, turn and leave rem 66 sts on holder.
Complete this side first. Dec one st at each end of every K row until 3 sts rem, ending with a P row.
Next row K2 tog, K1.
Next row P2 sts.
Next row K2 tog and fasten off.
With RS of work facing, sl first 29 sts on to holder and leave for yoke, rejoin yarn to rem 37 sts, K2 tog, K33 sts, K2 tog. Complete to match first side.

Left front
Using No.12 needles and A, cast on 50[52:54:56] sts. Work 4in K1, P1 rib. Change to No.10 needles. Beg with a K row cont in st st, inc one st at beg of 7th and every foll 8th row until there are 57[60:63:66] sts. Cont without shaping until work measures same as back to underarm, ending at armhole edge.
Shape armhole
Cast off 6 sts at beg of next row. 51[54:57:60] sts.
36, 38 and 40in sizes only
Next row P to end.
Next row K2 tog, K to end.
Rep last 2 rows until 51 sts rem for front yoke.
All sizes
Next row P14 sts and leave on holder, P37 sts.
Next row K2 tog, K to last 2 sts, K2 tog.
Next row P to end.
Rep last 2 rows until 3 sts rem. Complete as given for back.

Right front
Work as given for left front, reversing all shaping.

Sleeves
Using No.12 needles and A, cast on 58[60:62:64] sts. Work 4½in K1, P1 rib. Change to No.10 needles. Beg with a K row cont in st st, inc one st at each end of 5th and every foll 6th row until there are 84[90:96:102] sts. Cont in st st without shaping until sleeve measures 18½[19½:20½:21½]in from beg, or required length to underarm allowing 2in for turn back cuff, ending with a P row.
Shape top
Cast off 6 sts at beg of next 2 rows. 72[78:84:90] sts.
Next row K2 tog, K to last 2 sts, K2 tog.
Next row P to end.
Rep last 2 rows until 36 sts rem. Leave sts on holder for yoke.

Yoke
Join raglan seams. Using No.10 needles, A and with RS of work facing, K14 sts from right front holder, K up 28[31:34:37] sts up right neck edge, K36 sts from sleeve holder, K up 28[31:34:37] sts down right back neck, K29 sts from centre back holder, K up 28[31:34:37] sts up left back neck, K36 sts from sleeve holder, K up 28[31:34:37] sts down left front neck and K14 sts from left front holder. 241[253:265:277] sts.
Next row P to end, inc one st at centre back. 242[254:266:278] sts.
Next row Work from Chart 1 as foll, *K2 B, K2 A, rep from * to last 2 sts, K2 B.
Next row *P2 A, P2 B, rep from * to last 2 sts, P2 A.
Using A and beg with a K row work 2 rows st st, dec one st at centre back. 241[253:265:277] sts.

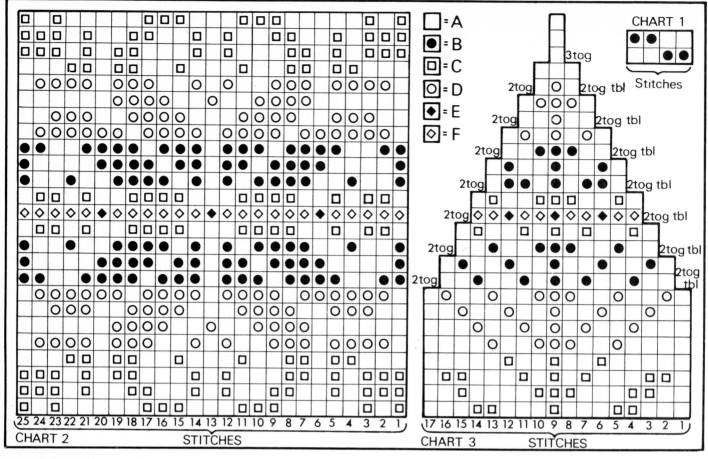

CHART 1 — Stitches

CHART 2 — STITCHES 25 24 23 22 21 20 19 18 17 16 15 14 13 12 11 10 9 8 7 6 5 4 3 2 1

CHART 3 — STITCHES 17 16 15 14 13 12 11 10 9 8 7 6 5 4 3 2 1

Key:
□ = A
● = B
▣ = C
○ = D
◆ = E
◇ = F

Cont in Fair Isle patt, working from charts as foll:

34, 36 and 38in sizes only
Omit first 18[12:6] sts of Chart 2 and beg on 19th [13th:7th] st of Chart 2, K rem 7[13:19] sts of Chart 2, K full patt of 42 sts of Charts 3 and 2 five times, then K17 sts of Chart 3 once, then K first 7[13:19] sts of Chart 2.
Cont working rem 24 rows of Charts, taking care to beg K rows on the 19th[13th:7th] sts and all P rows on the 7th[13th:19th] sts at front edge.

40in size only
Working from Charts, K 1st row of Chart 2, foll by 1st row of Chart 3 right across work, ending with 25 sts of Chart 2.

All sizes
Note that the dec on Chart 3 on 9th and foll alt rows are made by K first 2 sts tbl.
When 25 rows of Charts have been worked, break off all colours except A and the colour used for Chart 1.
Next row Using A, P to end.
Next row Using A, K10[7:4:1] sts, *K2 tog, K1, rep from * to last 9[6:3:0] sts, K2 tog, K7[K2 tog, K4: K2 tog, K1: K0]. 102[108:114:120] sts.
Beg with a P row work 2 rows of Chart 1. Cont using A only.
Next row P to end.
Next row K1[2:2:2] sts, *K2 tog, K3, rep from * to last 1[1:2:3] sts, K1[1:2:3]. 82[87:92:97] sts.
Change to No.12 needles. Work 2in K1, P1 rib. Cast off loosely in rib. Fold ribbing in half to WS and sl st cast off edge to 1st row of ribbing.

Button band
Using No.12 needles and A, cast on 11 sts.
1st row *K1, P1, rep from * to last st, K1.
Rep this row until band is same length as front edge when slightly stretched. Cast off. Sew on button band and mark positions for 10 buttons, first to come ½in above cast on edge and last to come ½in below cast off edge.

Buttonhole band
Work as given for button band, making buttonholes

as markers are reached, as foll:
Next row Moss st 4, cast off 3 sts, moss st 4.
Next row Work in moss st to end, casting on 3 sts above those cast off in previous row.

To make up
Press each piece under a damp cloth with a warm iron. Join side and sleeve seams.
Press seams.
Sew on buttons.

40 Jersey with Fair Isle yoke

Sizes
To fit 34[36:38:40]in bust
Length to shoulder, 21½[22:22½:23]in
Long sleeve seam, 16½[17½:18½:19½]in
Short sleeve seam, 4½[5:5½:6]in
The figures in brackets [] refer to the 36, 38 and 40in sizes respectively

Tension
As given for cardigan (design 39)

Materials
H & O Shetland Fleece distributed by Templetons
Long sleeved version 10[11:11:12] balls main shade, A
Short sleeved version 6[7:8:9] balls main shade, A
See materials for cardigan for contrast colours
One pair No.10 needles
One pair No.12 needles
One set of 4 No.10 needles pointed at both ends
One 4½in zip fastener

Front
Work as given for back of cardigan.

Back
Using No.12 needles and A, cast on 108[112:116:

120] sts and work as given for cardigan back until there are 114[120:126:132] sts. Cont without shaping until work measures 15in from beg, ending with a P row.

Shape armholes
Work as given for cardigan back until 102 sts rem. Work shaping as given for cardigan back, leaving 28 sts for yoke.

Short sleeves
Using No.12 needles and A, cast on 78[80:82:84] sts. Work 1in K1, P1 rib. Change to No.10 needles. Beg with a K row cont in st st, inc one st at each end of 3rd and every foll 4th row until there are 84[90:96:102] sts. Cont without shaping until sleeve measures 4½[5:5½:6]in from beg, ending with a P row.
Shape top
Work as given for top of cardigan sleeve.

Long sleeves
Work as given for sleeves of cardigan.

Yoke
Join raglan seams. With RS of work facing leave first 14 sts of back on holder. Using first needle of set of 4 No.10 needles and A, beg at centre back and K rem 14 sts of back, K up 28[31:34:37] sts up left back neck, K36 sts from sleeve, using 2nd needle K up 28[31:34:37] sts down left front neck, K29 sts from centre front holder, K up 28[31:34:37] sts up right neck, using 3rd needle K36 sts from other sleeve, K up 28[31:34:37] sts down right back neck, then K rem 14 sts from centre back neck. 241[253:265:277] sts.
Work as given for cardigan yoke until neckband is reached. Change to No.12 needles. Work 8 rows K1, P1 rib.
Cast off loosely in rib.

To make up
Press as given for cardigan. Join side and sleeve seams. Press seams. Sew back opening leaving 4½in open for zip. Sew in zip.

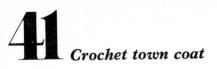

41 Crochet town coat

Sizes
To fit 34[36:38:40]in bust
36[38:40:42]in hips
Length to shoulder, 35[35½:36:36½]in
Sleeve seam, 14in
The figures in brackets [] refer to the 36, 38 and
40in sizes respectively

Tension
6 sts and 4 rows to 1in over htr worked on No 3·00
(ISR) crochet hook

Materials
25[28:30:33] balls Emu Scotch 4 ply
One No.3·00 (ISR) crochet hook

Back
Using No.3·00 (ISR) hook make 125[131:137:143]
ch.
1st row Into 3rd ch from hook work 1htr, 1htr in
each ch to end. Turn. 123[129:135:141] sts.
2nd row 2ch to count as first htr, 1htr into each
htr to end.
The 2nd row forms patt. Cont in patt until work
measures 9in from beg.
Shape sides
Dec one st at each end of next and every foll 8th
row until 113[119:125:131] sts rem. Cont without
shaping until work measures 18in from beg.
** **Next row** 3ch, miss first htr, *1tr in next st, 1ch,
miss one st, rep from * ending with 1 tr in turning
ch. Turn.
Work 3 rows in htr. **
Rep from ** to ** 7 times more, then cont in htr
until work measures 27in from beg.
Shape armholes
Next row Ss over first 4 sts, patt to last 4 sts, turn.
Dec one st at each end of every row until 33[35:37:
39] sts rem.
Fasten off.

Left front
Using No.3·00 (ISR) hook make 68[72:76:80] ch.
Work in patt as given for back until work measures
9in from beg. 66[70:74:78] sts.
Shape side
Dec one st at beg of next and every foll 8th row until
61[65:69:73] sts rem. Cont as given for back until
8th line of openwork st has been worked, ending at
front edge.
Shape dart
Next row Patt to last 7[7:8:8] sts, turn and patt
to end. Turn.
Next row Patt to last 14[14:16:16] sts, turn and
patt to end. Turn.
Next row Patt to last 21[21:24:24] sts, turn and
patt to end. Turn.
Next row Patt to last 28[28:32:32] sts, turn and
patt to end. Turn.
Cont without shaping until work measures same as
back to underarm, ending at armhole edge.
Shape armhole
Next row Ss over first 4 sts, patt to end. Turn.
Dec one st at armhole edge on every row until
31[33:35:37] sts rem, ending at front edge.
Shape neck
Next row Ss over first 10[12:12:14] sts, patt to
last 2 sts, dec one st. Turn.
Next row Dec one st, patt to last 2[2:3:3] sts, turn.
Next row Ss over first 2[2:3:3] sts, patt to last 2 sts,
dec one st. Turn.
Dec one st at each end of next 5 rows, then cont
dec at armhole edge only twice more. 2 sts. Fasten
off.

Right front
Work as given for left front, reversing all shaping.

Sleeves
Using No.3·00 (ISR) hook make 55[59:63:67] ch.
Work 4 rows htr as given for back. 53[57:61:65] sts.
Next row 3ch, miss first htr, *1tr in next st, 1ch,
miss one st, rep from * ending with 1tr in turning ch.
Turn.
Work 3 rows htr.
Rep patt row, then work 3 rows htr, inc one st at
each end of 2nd row of htr. Rep patt row once
more. Cont in htr, inc one st at each end of next and
every foll 3rd row until there are 79[83:87:91] sts.
Cont without shaping until sleeve measures 14in
from beg. Mark each end of last row with coloured
thread. Work 4 more rows.
Shape top
Dec one st at each end of every row until 7 sts rem.
Fasten off.

Pockets (make 2)
Using No.3·00 (ISR) hook make 33 ch. Work 15
rows htr as given for back. (Work openwork patt
row, then work 3 rows htr) twice, then work patt
row once more and 2 rows of htr. Fasten off.

To make up
Press each piece under a damp cloth with a warm
iron. Join raglan seams, sewing last 4 rows of sleeve
from markers to cast off sts at underarm. Join side
and sleeve seams. Using No.3·00 (ISR) hook and
with RS of work facing, work 5 rows dc along right
and left front edges.
Collar Using No.3·00 (ISR) hook and with WS of
work facing, rejoin yarn to beg of neck, 2ch, work
90[92:94:96] htr around neck edge. Turn. Work
2 rows htr.
Next row 2ch, work 20[20:21:21] htr, *2htr in
next st, 1htr in next st, 2htr in next st, work 20[21:
21:22] htr, rep from * once more, 2htr in next st,
1htr in next st, 2htr in next st, work 21[21:22:22]
htr. Turn.
Work 2 rows without shaping.
Next row 2ch, work 21[21:22:22] htr, *2htr in
next st, 1htr in next st, 2htr in next st, work 22[23:
23:24] htr, rep from * once more, 2htr in next st,
1htr in next st, 2htr in next st, work 22[22:23:23]
htr. Turn.
Work 2 rows without shaping.
Cont inc in this way on next and foll 3rd row.
Work 2 rows without shaping. Fasten off. With RS
of collar facing work a row dc round edges, turn
and work a 2nd row. Fasten off. Sew on pockets.
Press all seams.

42 Crochet town suit

Sizes
To fit 34[36:38:40]in bust
36[38:40:42]in hips
Jacket length to shoulder, 21½[22:22½:23]in
Sleeve seam, 17in
Skirt length, 21½[22:22½:23]in
The figures in brackets [] refer to the 36, 38 and
40in sizes respectively

Tension
5 sts and 2¾ rows to 1in over patt worked on
No.4·00 (ISR) crochet hook

Materials
32[34:37:39] balls Wendy Nylonised Double
Knitting in main shade, A
4[5:5:6] balls in contrast colour, B
One No.4·00 (ISR) crochet hook
12 buttons
Waist length of elastic
One 8in zip fastener

Skirt back
Using No.4·00 (ISR) hook and A, make 66[72:78:
84] ch and beg at waist.
1st row Into 3rd ch from hook work 1dc, *1ch,
miss 1ch, 1dc in next ch, rep from * to end. Turn.
65[71:77:83] sts.
2nd row 3ch, *1dc in next dc, 1ch, rep from *
ending with 1dc in turning ch. Turn.
The 2nd row forms patt and is rep throughout.
Work 2 more rows in patt. Place coloured marker at
each side of centre 27[29:31:33] sts.
Shape darts
Next row 3ch, work 1dc in same st to inc 2 sts,
1ch, 1dc in next dc,, rep from * to first marker,
(1ch, 1dc) twice into next st, rep from * to * to st
before next marker, (1ch, 1dc) twice into next st,
patt to end, ending with 1dc, 1ch, 1dc into turning
ch. Turn.
Cont to inc in this way on every foll 10th row
3 times more. 97[103:109:115] sts. Cont without
shaping until work measures 21½[22:22½:23]in
from beg.
Fasten off.

Skirt front
Work as given for back.

To make up
Press each piece under a damp cloth with a warm
iron. Join side seams leaving 8in open at top of left
seam for zip. Sew in zip. Sew elastic inside waist
edge with casing st.
Press seams.

Jacket back
Using No.4·00 (ISR) hook and A, make 90[96:102:
108] ch. Work in patt as given for skirt until work
measures 14in from beg. 89[95:101:107] sts.
Shape armholes
Next row Ss over first 6[6:8:8] sts, 3ch, patt to
last 6[6:8:8] sts, turn.
Dec 2 sts at each end of next and foll 2[3:3:4] alt
rows. 65[67:69:71] sts. Cont without shaping until
armholes measure 7½[8:8½:9]in from beg.
Shape neck and shoulders
Next row Ss over first 7[7:7:8] sts, patt 17[18:18:
18] sts, turn.
Next row Ss over first 2 sts, patt to last 7[8:8:8] sts.
Fasten off.
Miss first 17[17:19:19] sts, rejoin yarn to rem sts,
patt to last 7[7:7:8] sts, turn.
Next row Ss over first 7[8:8:8] sts, patt to last
2 sts. Fasten off.

Jacket left front
Using No.4·00 (ISR) hook and A, make 36[38:42:
44] ch. Work in patt as given for skirt until work
measures same as jacket back to underarm.
35[37:41:43] sts.
Shape armhole
Next row Ss over first 6[6:8:8] sts, patt to end. Turn.
Work 1 row. Dec 2 sts at armhole edge on next and
foll 2[3:3:4] alt rows. 23[23:25:25] sts. Cont
without shaping until armhole measures same as
back to shoulder, ending at armhole edge.
Shape shoulder
Next row Ss over first 7[7:7:8] sts, patt to end.
Turn.
Next row Patt to last 7[8:8:8] sts. Fasten off.

Left front band
Using No.4·00 (ISR) hook and B, with RS of work
facing beg at neck edge, miss first 6[6:7:7] row ends,
join in yarn to next row end, 3ch, *miss 1 row end,
1dc in next row end, 1ch, rep from * to end, ending
with 1dc in last row end. Turn. Cont in patt, dec
2 sts at neck edge on next and foll 2 alt rows, then
on foll row. Cont without shaping until 18[20:20:
22] rows have been worked, then inc 2 sts at neck
edge on next 2 rows, then on foll 2 alt rows. Fasten
off. Mark positions for 10 buttons, the first 2
buttons ¾in above lower edge and the last 2
buttons 3in below neck edge, with 3 more sets of
2 buttons evenly spaced between.

Jacket right front

Work as given for left front reversing all shapings.

Right front band

Work as given for left front band, beg at lower edge and making buttonholes on 4th and foll 20th[22nd:22nd:24th] row as foll: work in patt until marker is reached, 2ch, miss 1ch, 1dc, 1ch.
Next row Patt to end, working 1dc into each 2ch loop on previous row.

Sleeves

Using No.4·00 (ISR) hook and A, make 44[46:48:50] ch. Work 2 in patt as given for back. 43[45:47:49] sts. Inc 2 sts at each end of next and every foll 10th row until there are 67[69:71:73] sts. Cont without shaping until sleeve measures 17in from beg.
Shape top
Next row Ss over first 6[6:8:8] sts, patt to last 6[6:8:8] sts, turn.
Work 3 rows without shaping. Dec 2 sts at beg of every row until 11 sts rem. Fasten off.

Collar

Using No.4·00 (ISR) hook and B, make 86[88:90:92] ch. Work 4 rows patt. 85[87:89:91] sts.
Next row Patt 14 sts, work 1dc, 1ch, 1dc all into next st, patt to last 15 sts, work 1dc, 1ch, 1dc all into next st, patt to end.
Work 2 rows patt.
Rep last 3 rows 4 times more. Fasten off.

Cuffs

Using No.4·00 (ISR) hook and B, make 44[46:48:50] ch. Work 4 rows patt. Inc 2 sts at each end of next and every foll 3rd row 3 times in all. Work 2 rows after last inc row. Fasten off.

To make up

Press as given for skirt. Join shoulder seams. Set in sleeves. Join side and sleeve seams. Sew on collar and cuffs. Turn cuffs back over sleeves, sew one button to centre of outer side and make button loop on inner side to correspond. Press all seams. Sew on buttons to left front. Sew press stud to top corner of right front under collar if required.

43 *Back buttoning evening cardigan*

Sizes

To fit 34[36:38]in bust
Length to shoulder, 20in adjustable
Sleeve seam, 16½in adjustable
The figures in brackets [] refer to the 36 and 38in sizes respectively

Tension

6 sts and 9 rows to 1in over main patt worked on No.9 needles

Materials

15[16:17] balls of Twilley's Goldfingering
One pair No.9 needles
One pair No.10 needles
One pair No.11 needles
One each circular needles No.9, No.10 and No.11
14 buttons

Front

Using No.11 needles cast on 111[119:127] sts. Work 10 rows K1, P1 rib. Change to No.9 needles.
Commence main patt.
1st row K2 sts, *yfwd, K2 tog, rep from * to last st, K1.
This row forms main patt. Cont in patt until work measures 13in from beg, or required length to underarm, ending with a WS row.
Shape armholes
Cast off 6[8:8] sts at beg of next 2 rows. Dec one st

at each end of next 6[8:10] RS rows.
Work 1 row.
Leave rem 87[87:91] sts on holder.

Left back

Using No.11 needles cast on 60[64:68] sts.
1st row K6 sts, *P1, K1, rep from * to end.
2nd row *P1, K1, rep from * to last 6 sts, P1, K5 sts.
Rep these 2 rows 3 times more, then 1st row once.
Next row Work in rib until 5 sts rem, turn leaving rem 5 sts on holder for front band. 55[59:63] sts.
** Change to No.9 needles. Work in patt as given for back until work measures same as back to underarm, ending at armhole edge.
Shape armhole
Cast off 6[8:8] sts at beg of next row. Dec one st at armhole edge on next 6[8:10] alt rows.
Work 1 row.
Leave rem 43[43:45] sts on holder. **

Right back

Using No 11 needles cast on 60[64:68] sts.
1st row *K1, P1, rep from * to last 6 sts, K6.
2nd row K5 sts, P1, *K1, P1, rep from * to end.
Rep these 2 rows 3 times more, then 1st row once.
Next row K5 sts and leave these sts on holder, rib to end.
Complete as given for left back from ** to **.

Sleeves

Using No.11 needles cast on 57[61:67] sts. Work 2in K1, P1 rib. Work main patt as given for front until work measures 3in from beg. Change to No.10 needles and cont in main patt until work measures 4in from beg. Change to No 9 needles and cont in main patt, inc one st at each end of 9th and every foll 8th row 8[10:10] times in all, then on every foll 12th row 4 times in all. 81[89:95] sts.
Cont in main patt without shaping until sleeve measures 16½in from beg, or required length to underarm.
End with a WS row.
Shape top
Cast off 6[8:8] sts at beg of next 2 rows. Dec one st at each end of next 6[8:10] RS rows. Work 1 row.
Leave rem 57[57:59] sts on holder.

Yoke

34 and 36in sizes only
1st row Using No 9 circular needle, across 43 sts of left back K2, (yfwd, K2 tog) 20 times then sl rem st on to beg of 57 sts of one sleeve, yfwd, K3 tog, (yfwd, K2 tog) 27 times, yfwd, K1, across 87 sts of front (yfwd, K2 tog) 43 times then sl rem st on to beg of 57 sts of 2nd sleeve, yfwd, K3 tog, (yfwd, K2 tog) 27 times, yfwd, K1, across 43 sts of right back (yfwd, K2 tog) 21 times, K last st. 287 sts.
Work 3 rows main patt.
38in size only
1st row Using No 9 circular needle, across 45 sts of left back K2, (yfwd, K2 tog) 21 times, yfwd, K1, across the 59 sts of one sleeve (yfwd, K2 tog) 29 times, yfwd, K1, across 91 sts of front (yfwd, K2 tog) 45 times, yfwd, K1, across 59 sts of 2nd sleeve (yfwd, K2 tog) 29 times, yfwd, K1, across 45 sts of right back (yfwd, K2 tog) 22 times, K1. 303 sts.
Work 3 rows main patt, inc one st in 2nd st, one st in centre and one st in 2nd st from end of last row. 306 sts.
All sizes
Commence yoke patt.
1st row K1, *sl 1, K1, psso, K3, (yfwd, sl 1, K1, psso) twice, yfwd, K1, yfwd, (K2 tog, yfwd) twice, K3, K2 tog, rep from * to last st, K1.
2nd and every alt row P to end.
3rd, 5th and 7th rows As 1st row.
9th row K1, *sl 1, K1, psso, K2, (yfwd, K2 tog) twice, yfwd, K3, yfwd, (sl 1, K1, psso, yfwd) twice, K2, K2 tog, rep from * to last st, K1.
11th row K1, *sl 1, K1, psso, K1, (yfwd, K2 tog) twice, yfwd, K5, yfwd, (sl 1, K1, psso, yfwd) twice, K1, K2 tog, rep from * to last st, K1.

13th row K1, *sl 1, K1, psso, (yfwd, K2 tog) twice, yfwd, K7, yfwd, (sl 1, K1, psso, yfwd) twice, K2 tog, rep from * to last st, inc one in last st.
15th row *Sl 1, K1, psso, (yfwd, K2 tog) twice, yfwd, K3, K2 tog, K4, yfwd, (sl 1, K1, psso, yfwd) twice, rep from * to last 3 sts, sl 1, K1, psso, K1.
16th row P to end.
Change to No 10 circular needle.
17th row K1, *(yfwd, K2 tog) twice, yfwd, K3, K2 tog, sl 1, K1, psso, K3, yfwd, (sl 1, K1, psso, yfwd) twice, K1, rep from * to last st, K1.
19th, 21st and 23rd rows As 17th row.
25th row K1, *K1, (yfwd, sl 1, K1, psso) twice, yfwd, K2, K2 tog, sl 1, K1, psso, K2, (yfwd, K2 tog) twice, yfwd, K2, rep from * to last st, K1.
27th row K1, *K2, (yfwd, sl 1, K1, psso) twice, yfwd, K1, K2 tog, sl 1, K1, psso, K1, yfwd, (K2 tog, yfwd) twice, K3, rep from * to last st, K1.
29th row K1, *K3, (yfwd, sl 1, K1, psso) twice, yfwd, K2 tog, sl 1, K1, psso, yfwd, (K2 tog, yfwd) twice, K4, rep from * to last st, K1.
31st row K1, *K4, (yfwd, sl 1, K1, psso) 3 times, yfwd, (K2 tog, yfwd) twice, K3, K2 tog, rep from * to last st, K1.
32nd row P to end.
Change to No.11 circular needle. Rep 1st to 7th patt rows once more.
1st dec row P5, *P2 tog, P2 tog, P3, P2 tog, P2 tog, P8, rep from * ending last rep P5. 227[227:242] sts.
2nd dec row K1, sl 1, K1, psso, K4, *sl 1, K2 tog, psso, K5, sl 1, K1, psso, K5, rep from * to last 10 sts, sl 1, K2 tog, psso, K4, sl 1, K1, psso, K1. 181[181:193] sts.
1st rib row K2, *P1, K1, rep from * to last st, K1.
2nd rib row K1, *P1, K1, rep from * to end.
Rep these 2 rows twice more.
3rd dec row K2, *sl 1, P2 tog, psso, rib 5, rep from * to last 3[3:7] sts, P1, K2[P1, K2: rib 5, K2].
Work 7 rows rib.
4th dec row K2, P1, K1, *sl 1, K2 tog, psso, rib 7, rep from * to last 3 sts, P1, K2. 111[111:119] sts. Work 4 rows rib. Mark each end of last row with coloured thread.
Work collar
Cont in rib on these sts for a further 11in. Cast off in rib.

Button band

Using No.11 needles and with WS of work facing rejoin yarn to 5 sts left on holder of left back and cont in g st until band is long enough, when slightly stretched, to fit up centre back edge to coloured marker. Do not cast off. Mark positions for 11 buttons, first to come 4 rows below sts on needle and rem 10 at 2in intervals. Cont in g st for a further 11in to match edge of collar.
Cast off.
Sew on band.

Buttonhole band

Using No.11 needles and with RS of work facing rejoin yarn to 5 sts left on holder of right back and work as given for button band making first 11 buttonholes as markers are reached as foll:
Buttonhole row K1, cast off 2 sts, K2.
Next row K2, cast on 2 sts, K1.
When 11th buttonhole has been worked, K2 rows g st, when band should reach coloured marker.
Work 1in g st.
** Work 2 buttonhole rows, then work 2in g st.** Rep from ** to ** once more. Work 2 buttonhole rows then work 1in g st. Rep from ** to ** twice more. Work 2 buttonhole rows then work 1in g st.
Cast off.
Sew on band.

To make up

Do not press. Set in sleeves. Join side and sleeve seams. Fold collar in half to RS so that 3 double buttonholes match. Neaten buttonholes. Sew on buttons.

Cocktail suit

Sizes
To fit 34[36:38:40:42]in bust
36[38:40:42:44]in hips
Jacket length to shoulder, 23[23½:24:24½:25]in
Sleeve seam, 6in
Skirt length, 20[20½:21:21½:22]in
The figures in brackets [] refer to the 36, 38, 40
and 42in sizes respectively

Tension
7 sts and 9 rows to 1in over st st worked on No.10
needles

Materials
22[24:26:28:30] balls Lister Bel Air Starspun
One pair No.10 needles
One pair No.12 needles
Six buttons
Waist length of elastic
One 7in zip fastener

Jacket back
Using No.12 needles cast on 123[129:137:143:151]
sts.
1st row K1, *P1, K1, rep from * to end.
2nd row P1, *K1, P1, rep from * to end.
Rep these 2 rows for 1in, ending with a 2nd row and
inc one st at end of last row on 36 and 40in sizes
only. 123[130:137:144:151] sts.
Change to No.10 needles. Beg with a K row cont in
st st until work measures 16in from beg, ending
with a P row.
Shape armholes
Cast off at beg of next and every row 6 sts twice and
2[2:3:3:4] sts 4 times. Dec one st at each end of
next and foll 5[7:7:9:9] alt rows. 91[94:97:100:
103] sts. Cont without shaping until armholes
measure 7[7½:8:8½:9]in from beg, ending with a
P row.
Shape neck and shoulders
Next row K30[31:32:33:34] sts, turn and leave
rem sts on holder.
Next row Cast off 4 sts, P to end.
Next row Cast off 6[6:7:7:7] sts, K to end.
Rep last 2 rows once more, then first of them once
more. Cast off rem 6[7:6:7:8] sts.
With RS of work facing, sl first 31[32:33:34:35] sts
on holder, rejoin yarn to rem sts and K to end.
Complete to match first side, reversing shaping.

Jacket left front
Using No.12 needles cast on 75[79:83:87:91] sts.
1st row *K1, P1, rep from * to last 21 sts, K10,
sl 1, K10.
2nd row P21 sts, *K1, P1, rep from * to end.
Rep these 2 rows for 1in, ending with a 2nd row.
Change to No.10 needles.
Next row K to last 11 sts, sl 1, K10.
Next row P to end.
Rep last 2 rows until work measures same as back
to underarm, ending at armhole edge.
Shape armhole
Cast off at beg of next and foll alt rows 6 sts once
and 2[2:3:3:4] sts twice, ending at armhole edge.
Shape neck
Next row K2 tog, K to last 29[30:31:32:33] sts,
turn and leave rem sts on holder.
Dec one st at armhole edge on foll 5[7:7:9:9] alt
rows, *at the same time* cast off at neck edge on next and
foll alt rows 4 sts once, 3 sts once, 2 sts once and one
st 3 times. 18[19:20:21:22] sts. Cont without
shaping until armhole measures same as back to
shoulder, ending at armhole edge.
Shape shoulder
Cast off at beg of next and every alt row 6[6:7:7:7]
sts twice and 6[7:6:7:8] sts once. Mark positions
for 6 buttons, the first to come ½in above hem and

last to come in neckband ½in above sts on holder,
with 4 more evenly spaced between.

Jacket right front
Using No.12 needles cast on 75[79:83:87:91] sts.
1st row K10, sl 1, K10, *P1, K1, rep from * to end.
2nd row *P1, K1, rep from * to last 21 sts, P21.
Rep these 2 rows once more.
Next row (buttonhole row) K3 sts, cast off 4 sts,
K2, sl 1, K3, cast off 4 sts, patt to end.
Next row Patt to end, casting on 4 sts above those
cast off in previous row.
Complete to match left front, reversing all shaping
and making buttonholes as markers are reached, as
before.

Sleeves
Using No.12 needles cast on 69[73:77:81:85] sts.
Work 1in rib as given for back, ending with a 2nd
row. Change to No.10 needles. Beg with a K row
cont in st st, inc one st at each end of 5th and every
foll 6th row until there are 83[87:91:95:99] sts.
Cont without shaping until sleeve measures 6in
from beg, ending with a P row.
Shape top
Cast off 6 sts at beg of next 2 rows. Dec one st at
each end of next and foll 11[12:13:14:15] alt rows.
Cast off at beg of next and every row 2 sts 10[10:12:
12:14] times, 3 sts 4 times and 4 sts twice. Cast off
rem 7[9:7:9:7] sts.

Neckband
Join shoulder seams. Using No.12 needles and with
RS of work facing, patt across sts of right front neck,
K up 45 sts up side of front neck and 20 sts down
side of back neck, K across back neck sts inc one st
in centre on 36 and 40in sizes only, K up 20 sts up
side of back neck and 45 sts down side of front neck,
patt across sts of left front neck. 219[223:225:229:
231] sts.
Next row P21 sts, rib to last 21 sts, P21.
Next row K10, sl 1, K10, rib to last 21 sts, K10,
sl 1, K10.
Rep last 2 rows for 1in making buttonholes as
before on 5th and 6th rows. Cast off in patt.

To make up
Press lightly under a dry cloth with a cool iron. Set
in sleeves. Join side and sleeve seams. Fold front
bands in half to WS and sl st down. Work round
double buttonholes. Press seams. Sew on buttons.

Skirt back
Using No.12 needles cast on 91[97:105:111:119]
sts and beg at waist. Work 1in rib as given for
jacket back, ending with a 2nd row and inc one st
at end of last row on 36 and 40in sizes only. 91[98:
105:112:119] sts. Change to No.10 needles.
Beg with a K row work 4 rows st st.
Shape darts
Next row K14 sts, pick up loop between sts and
K tbl – called inc 1 –, K19[21:23:25:27] sts, inc 1,
K25[28:31:34:37] sts, inc 1, K19[21:23:25:27] sts,
inc 1, K14 sts.
Beg with a P row work 9 rows st st.
Next row K14 sts, inc 1, K20[22:24:26:28] sts, inc
1, K27[30:33:36:39] sts, inc 1, K20[22:24:26:28]
sts, inc 1, K14 sts.
Beg with a P row work 9 rows st st.
Cont inc in this way on next and every foll 10th row
until there are 143[150:157:164:171] sts.
Cont without shaping until work measures 20[20½:
21:21½:22]in from beg, ending with a P row and
inc one st at end of last row on 36 and 40in sizes
only.
Next row (picot edge) K1, *yfwd, K2 tog, rep
from * to end.
Change to No.12 needles. Beg with a P row work
1½in st st. Cast off.

Skirt front
Work as given for back.

To make up
Press as given for jacket. Join side seams leaving 7in
open at top of left seam for zip. Turn hem to WS at
picot row and sl st down. Sew in zip. Sew elastic
inside waist ribbing with casing st. Press seams.

KNITTING AND CROCHET ABBREVIATIONS

alt	alternate(ly)
approx	approximate(ly)
beg	begin(ning)
ch	chain
cont	continu(e)(ing)
dec	decrease
dc	double crochet
dtr	double treble
foll	follow(ing)
g st	garter stitch, every row knit
gr(s)	group(s)
htr	half treble
in	inch(es)
inc	increase
K	knit
K up	pick up and knit
K-wise	knitwise
No.	number
psso	pass slipped stitch over
patt	pattern
P	purl
P up	pick up and purl
P-wise	purlwise
rem	remain(ing)
rep	repeat
RS	right side
sl	slip
sl st	slip stitch in knitting
ss	slip stitch in crochet
sp	space
st(s)	stitch(es)
st st	stocking stitch, 1 row knit, 1 row purl
tbl	through back of loop
tog	together
tr	treble
tr tr	triple treble
WS	wrong side
yd(s)	yard(s)
ybk	yarn back
yfwd	yarn forward
yon	yarn over needle
yrh	yarn round hook
yrn	yarn round needle

SYMBOLS

An asterisk, (*), shown in a pattern row denotes that the stitches shown after this sign must be repeated from that point.

Square brackets, [ ], denote instructions for larger sizes in the pattern. Round brackets, ( ), denote that this section of the pattern is to be worked for all sizes.

Crochet hooks have been standardized into an International Size range, (ISR), and these sizes will be used throughout these instructions.

Tension – this is the most important factor in successful knitting and crochet. Unless you obtain the tension given for each design, you will not obtain satisfactory results.